MAKER
LOVER
&KEEPER

The Art of Living and Loving

JAMES McDERMOTT

Mc Crimmons

Great Wakering, Essex

First published 1990 by McCrimmon Publishing Co Ltd.,
10–12 High Street, Great Wakering, Essex SS3 0EQ

© 1990 James W. McDermott

ISBN 0 85597 454 0

NIHIL OBSTAT   Rev. Timothy Russ M.A.
                             Censor Deputatus.

IMPRIMATUR   Rt. Rev. Francis Thomas S.T.L.
                             Episcopus Northantoniensis
                             die j Novembris 1987.

Cover design by Nick Snode
Typeset in Imprint, 12/13.5
Typesetting by Fleetlines, Southend
Printed by The Wolsey Press Ltd, Ipswich — 0473-719377

CONTENTS

'He showed me a little thing, the size of a hazelnut, in the palm of my hand, round as a ball. I looked at it prayerfully… In this little thing I saw three truths. The first is that God made it. The second is that God loves it. The third is that God keeps it in being. What is he who is in truth *Maker, Lover and Keeper*? Words can never tell. For until I am one with him, when I am held so close to him that there is nothing between us, I can never find true rest and lasting happiness'.

Mother Julian of Norwich.

PREFACE

MANY years ago I had the privilege of making a retreat under Canon J. Arendzen. I remember a story he told of how he was tempted to enter a fellow student's room at Oscott College, and how he found there a painting of an eye and under it the words 'God sees'. I have always believed that the secret to life lies in the ability to see. Later I came to realize that to see is also to love. Insight adds to the joy of living; the Psalmist was inspired to sing: 'I have more insight than all who teach me, for I ponder your will' (Ps. 119:100). Yet insight is difficult to analyse, it is far easier to paint or radiate than depict in limpid verbal expression. Words so often fail to present the deep reality of what is seen or felt. The hidden thought seems to fade as soon as it is put in words or transposed into dialect. St. Paul complained of this to the Corinthians (2 Cor. 4). Vision, I suppose, can only be met by vision. Pope John XXIII used to say: 'Read my heart, you will find more there than words'.

Our way of looking at things is conditioned by what we are. Most of us are faced with not a single truth but many, not one but several pictures of reality. Because of this we are conscious of a discord in our lives. And yet it has always been the quest of men and women to seek the one ultimate truth, the final synthesis, in which all partial truths are resolved. For St. Paul, as for the Christian, the problem is solved in 'the mystery' of Christ Jesus. Like Moses, our search is to see God face to face. St. Paul told the Corinthians that this is not just a vague hope, rather it comes about by a gradual transformation. 'And we all, with unveiled face, beholding the glory of the Lord, are being changed into his likeness from one degree of glory to another' (2 Cor. 3:18). Indeed, his early concept of Christ, expressed in his letter to the Galatians, was to grow into what he described in his old age at Rome as 'the Day of Christ, when you will reach the perfect goodness which Jesus Christ produces in us for the glory and praise of God' (Phil. 1:11).

There is so much in life that has beauty and often we only appreciate it in middle life, when projections are withdrawn, and we begin to find within ourselves all that we previously looked for outside. Again this was the experience of St. Paul. He began to see that Christ by virtue of his Incarnation became an integral part of our world, and that by sharing intimately in our activities he won it back to his Father; that by virtue of his Resurrection the Body of Christ became the organic centre of the world; that through the Eucharist and his presence in the Church, he was to assimilate to himself not only the human race, but the whole world. Indeed, creation and the Incarnation are still daily experiences. Each day the opportunity is given us to love Christ and to discover him more and more. Through grace, through life and love, Christ becomes extended over the whole of creation. Each of us has the unique task of self realization in our search for Christ, and our efforts and tenacity are so important. Without effort some part of being will never be achieved. Besides, our efforts help the rest of our fellow human beings as well.

There is in most us a certain wildness. In middle life I came to appreciate the passivities and the deeper, more rugged side of life, the apatheia, in the Christian sense, that nature portrays. The wild aspect of Charnwood with its Precambrian rocks held an attraction for me. I loved to roam in the bracken, growing neath the outcrops, with mysterious looking oaks scattered round. You have to push your way through the jungle of bracken, careful to miss the deep holes that the badgers dig. It is all so symbolic of the unconscious. Often paths lead upwards, as they should, to elevated outcrops. I would sit there on the top, looking down on the way I had come, at the vast expanse of Mother Earth, with her breasts rising and falling, and at the East Midlands Airfield in the distance, thinking of the Shaman, that birdlike figure, and my own transcendent journey.

The thoughts that follow stem from those days, thoughts that I was privileged to share with the late Dr. Franz Elkisch, pupil and friend of his master, Jung. The words found expression in recent years. For the most part they deal with the age-old problem of our desire for union, our search for at-one-ment (atonement). Creation was to lack perfection, for God alone is perfect, but our first parents did enjoy the beauty of an ordered life, with its harmony and unity, and lack of shame. Genesis goes out of its way to tell us: 'they felt no shame in front of each other' (Gen. 2:25). The rift came only after their disobedience, when they had eaten of the fruit of the tree of knowledge of good and evil. They became conscious that they were different, not only physically but also psychologically and spiritually. They knew they were separated from God and each other. Adam lost his love for his wife, and openly blamed her for his sin. All inner unity had gone and a sense of guilt and shame took its place.

It is 'in Christ' that all healing is restored and new life and love is recovered. It is only through him that we come to a communion with one another, since 'he holds all things in unity' (Col. 1:17). In the end, he tells us, we shall be judged by his 'new commandment', on our loving, and that loving, as in the Trinity itself, finds its expression in a oneness. Love is a relationship that is bound by a unity. But the mystery is we become one with the other by first discovering the inner oneness of ourselves. St. Mark tell us how well the Scribe who listened to Our Lord understood this. 'Well spoken, Master; what you have said is true: that he is one and there is no other. To love him… and to love your neighbour as yourself, this is far more important than any holocaust or sacrifice'. And this prompted Our Lord to reply: 'You are not far from the kingdom of God' (Mark 12:32–34).

Being a Christian for St. Paul meant far more than just professing a religious system of belief with its moral code and acts of worship. It was also to be a daily experience of living and loving in Christ. He was proud to boast of the fact that there was nothing 'that will outweigh the supreme advantage of knowing Christ Jesus my Lord' (Phil. 3:8). It seems to me that in our present age we need an optimism to help us see and love Christ in all our lives. This little work is concerned with that gentle art. The hands of Christ are always present to mould and create, those hands through which so great a love is experienced. With St. Paul we can become more convinced that through love Christ is everywhere. Dr. Jung might not have been a theologian, but he was able to trace an ever recurring pattern of the living Christ in the spirit of men and women. Our growth, through the collective unconscious, adds to the wonderful act of creation, and helps us to bring to life within us what Pope John Paul II calls 'the Redemption in practice'.

When all is said and done, it is the Word of God that will remain, the rest will fade away. God's Word is the message written on 'white stone' given by the Spirit, 'known to him only who receives it' (Rev. 2:17). What follows is influenced by a love of Sacred Scripture. I am very grateful to the English and Welsh Hierarchy and to A.P. Watt Ltd. for their kind permission to quote from *The Bible*, translated by Monsignor R. Knox, and to Darton, Longman and Todd Ltd. and Doubleday & Co. Inc. for their permission to quote from *The Jerusalem Bible* published and copyright 1966, 1967 and 1968, and also to The National Council of the Churches of Christ in the U.S.A. for permission to quote from the *Revised Standard Version Common Bible* copyrighted 1973.

There is nothing new under the sun, and I am conscious of all those who have influenced me, the many authors I have read, the people with whom I have lived, and all those who have helped to form and guide me. I treasure their thoughts that have become so much part of me, thoughts no doubt which will come out here. God bless them all.

James W. McDermott

PART ONE

LIVING AND LOVING

1

All that came to be had life in him.
(John 1:4)

CHRIST is so vast, no one person can ever reproduce or depict him. Christianity too can be lived in different ways in the wide expanse of the one Christ. It seems to me that it matters little what others may think. Our experiences are different. Thank God we are all so different. But we respect the attitudes of others; indeed we must. We have to be bold enough to live our own experiences to be true to ourselves. Like the Psalmist we can voice our praise: 'I thank you for the wonder of myself ' (Ps. 139:14).

There is so much in life that has wonder, and the strange thing is, we only see it as we develop. When we think of the great age of the earth and the planets and the slow movement of creation, is it not surprising that it takes time in our own lives before we see fully the line of its direction? It was impressed upon me from my youth, and sometimes with the rod: 'Omnis festinatio ex parte diaboli est' – haste is the devil's own work. Life is a movement we are led into over a long period. In fact all the past is a preparation for it. Life is like a star or planet that we are drawn to by the force of its magnetism, and then finally we come right up to, and see it in all its glory and brightness.

One of the most dangerous illusions that has invaded the heart of us all is the fallacy of our own completeness. We should develop; ideals change, sometimes vocations change, even though the Christ who resides there always remains the same. We all carry within us the turmoil of the world, the problems of life with all its despairs. Left to ourselves we all could lose heart. But Christianity can draw upon an added source of strength and we can always go forward. Ultimately, everything is held together from on high. This became so clear to me on seeing Ribalta's painting of Christ embracing St. Bernard, Abbot of Clairvaux, from the Crucifix. St. Paul, too, reminded the Corinthians that 'anyone who is joined to the Lord is one spirit with him' (1 Cor. 6:17). Faith and love are the only realities that transport us beyond what the eye has never seen or the ear heard. It is always the invisible that never ceases to attract us. We can only live fully in the hope of following Christ. His own submission to his Passion and Death found its climax in his Resurrection, the active force that overcomes all chaos and suffering. We could never live without him and the life he gives us in his Eucharistic Sacrifice, which makes us become what we receive.

It is sad to think of the countless numbers there are drugged by the conventional ideas and ways of living, that seem to close their eyes. We can and we should enjoy life to the full – all the beauty and all that has been created to excite the human heart – when we have found the living presence of Christ leaping from it. To grasp this secret we have to be animated fundamentally by a mystical hope. This is always born within, an archetype that can emerge, only there must be the right circumstances and the right attitude. In time, like St. Augustine, we come more close to it and express a little more freely what we feel and see, and then begin to live. He prayed: 'See Lord, I cast my care upon you, that I may live.'

2

Be glad and rejoice for ever.
(Isaiah 65:18)

SO FEW seem to enjoy the good things in life. Today the more leisure people get, the more pleasure they seem to need to fill it. It is the ability to surrender ourselves to the deeper side of life that gives a joy and pleasure to living and loving. Tension and stress are perfectly normal, and are met in any form of life. The danger is when we allow them to become overpowering. It is helpful to see and understand ourselves, to help ward off any danger of unconscious forces that can so easily destroy. A perfect ordered society with everyone living in effortless ease and comfort would never produce peace, but only tedium.

We do need confidence in our individual selves, that in spite of all we feel, all our weaknesses and uncertainties, we can carry on because God is with us. This helps to create a zest for living, and helps us to realize that regression and progression are the normal phases of life. We regress to progress. It is not our problems that count, but the way we face them. So often we come up against a wall, and all our beating against it does not help. The only thing to do is to look coolly at it and see how high it is. If it is too solid and too high and we cannot get round it, we must accept the situation, and try to see God on top of it. He will then lift us up. It is necessary to have faith, faith in God, faith in ourselves, faith in others and faith in the future. In spite of all, our roots stand firm and our branches spread out to the rest of the world. Humanity forms a single tree, and together we take in all that God gives, and breathe out life that is efficacious to those near and dear, and to all the world. 'The life I now live in this body I live in faith: faith in the Son of God who loved me and who sacrificed himself for my sake' (Gal. 2:20).

3

Love no flood can quench, no torrent drown.
(Song of Songs 8:7)

THE POWER to love is a liberating power. The writings of Herman Hesse, who died in 1962, are recognized as Modern Classics because of their lyrical style and depth of thought. There is a lovely story in his 'Demian', which Eva, symbol of the Eternal Mother, relates to Sinclair about how love finds its way to certainty. It is about a youth who fell in love with a star. This star became the object of his thought, so much so that one night, standing on a cliff gazing up into the heavens, he burned so much with love for it, that he leaped into space towards it. But just as he leaped he thought 'this is impossible', and lay shattered on the shore. Hesse says he had not understood how to love. He lacked the steadfast faith in the fulfilment and power of his love. Had he had this, he would have soared into space and been united with his star. Our Lord said something similar, when he told his Apostles that if they had faith they could remove mountains. 'Nothing will be impossible to you' (Matt. 17:20–21).

Love is an energy, and in our surrender we find not only the other, but also ourselves and everything that is. In the 'Paradiso' it was Beatrice who led Dante to the face of God, and in her eyes resting on God, he saw he had won not only a woman, but also the whole world. Love is an energy, and all energy must converge. All love should converge in Christ. In the last resort love, even when felt on the natural level, must be an encounter with God. He alone is capable of setting ablaze all that lies deep in the human heart, transforming and carrying it along. It is Christ himself that gives this certainty, who brings it to fulfilment. It is then that the infinite, transcending as it does man and woman, makes it possible to love with an eternal love. Christ does enter into all that is beautiful and most human in our lives.

Love has its own power and can never be isolated. Yet all the time we need to be free to love Christ. St. Augustine, who had such a wide experience of love, writing in his Enarratio on Psalm 121 said: 'If you want to know what your love is like, look to where it leads you'. His actual words are: 'Sed vis nosse qualis amor sit? Vide quo ducat'. Again he said: 'God calls out to us, "Love me and you will posses me, because you cannot love me unless you posses me" ' (Sermon 34).

4

Anyone who is joined to the Lord is one spirit with him.
(1 Cor. 6:17)

TALK of communication of our being is not just a figure of speech, but can become a tangible reality in our lives. It is a conviction that comes with prayerful repose, an experience of the passivities, and all that lies deep in our being. Immersed in ourselves we find a peace, a collectedness and presence of mind, without which no right work can be achieved.

An inward movement, a spirit of love, is initiated in which in a most secret and intimate way our whole being is directed in a spirit of transference. Just as a burning candle is used to light others with, so we can transfer the spirit of our being from heart to heart, that they may be illumined. We give and receive in a spirit of receptiveness. Indeed, 'we have all been given drink at a single source, the one Spirit' (1 Cor. 12:13). We have to dwell in this boundless truth to be sustained by it.

This is an art of our inner being. It is immaterial what name we give it, whether we name it at all. It comes from our being, and we can only be, something that springs from the depths of which the workaday world knows nothing, from the fountain of living waters welling from within. 'Do you

17

not understand that you are God's temple, and that God's Spirit has his dwelling in you?' (1 Cor. 3:16). It is an experience that comes with faith, an inner conviction, something that can become effortless, with unbroken equanimity, a conviction and acceptance we are never afraid to come back to every day.

The world is bathed in an inward light which intensifies its relief, its structure and its depth. It is not just a superficial glimmer, but a calm and powerful radiance centred 'in Christ'. There is nothing that does not emanate from God, depend upon him and is his sacrament. Faith reveals the living active reality of God in the world and history. Christ appears, is born daily in the heart of our world. We can train our sensitivity to God, and foster within ourselves this feeling, this appreciation and zest for the omnipresence that enfolds everything.

If we dare to believe we enter a sphere of the created, where objects retain their normal texture, yet become animated and loving. This gives an optimism that sees unity in all becoming. The face of God is seen in Christ, whose body is everywhere present. St. Paul reminds us: 'All of us, in union with Christ, form one body, and as parts of it we belong to each other' (Rom. 12, 5). And he goes on to say: 'The body grows until it has built itself up, in love' (Eph. 4:16). It is especially in love that the living presence of God is felt. 'As long as we love one another God will live in us' (1 John 4:12).

5

It is my prayer that your love may abound more and more.
(Phil. 1:9)

OUR LOVE for God and for what is right and just will always find its consummation in him. This love is an invisible zest given from heaven that can never be lost. For Christ does not destroy what he adopts, but rather transforms and builds up into himself.

It is good to realize that the whole day that is given us is ours. If we try to develop in it a calmness and peace we can achieve a power of concentration and presence of mind that is so helpful in creating a sense of well-being for doing what is good and right, especially in the practice of the art of loving, which is very much a productive activity. An inward movement and form of passivity is required to balance all that is extroverted in our lives. We then begin to see that it is not necessary to seek, rather we find. Like the showers of rain falling from the sky, the waves rolling on the ocean, the stars and moon shining at night, the green foliage shooting forth in the spring, it is all so effortless, and yet directed by a force of love. Nature does not analyse itself; it is, and its being and becoming radiate love and enchantment. The sun loves the flower and the flower the sun.

In the winter months in the past, until I began to find, I used to become frantic. I love the snow with its virginal whiteness, and yet I could see all my shrubs being bent down under its weight, all prostrate, as it were, in adoration, touching the ground. I feared they would all snap, and the branches break and the natural shape be spoilt, destroyed by the Great Mother. The frost brought the sun, and then suddenly the snow would gently melt and slide off the foliage. The branches did not spring back at once, as if released from tension, but gradually the light would draw them upright, and almost imperceptibly they would right themselves. Nature knows this, it loves. It can remain calm because it accepts and bows down, and knows that it will rise again. It lives and loves in unbroken equanimity.

6

It is he who gives everything – including life and breath – to everyone.
(Acts 17:25)

WE SHOULD always pray for the passion for living, since it is the breath of God that has been breathed into us. His breath is the Spirit that energizes and creates new life. 'Then he breathed into his nostrils a breath of life, and thus man became a living being' (Gen. 2:7). Significant too is the fact that after his Resurrection, on the first day of the week, Our Lord came to his disciples and said to them: ' "Peace be with you"... After saying this he breathed on them' (John 20:21–22).

We live because we breathe. Correct breathing is a wonderful help to living and loving. It creates a calm and peace and can become the main source of our spiritual strength, flowing into our whole being. Eastern mysticism sees the secret of correct breathing as an artless art. To develop this art it is necessary for a few minutes each day to concentrate entirely on breathing, listening to ourselves breathing gently out and in, as if we had nothing else to do. Eventually we learn to lose ourselves so effortlessly in breathing, that we feel we are not breathing, but strange as it might sound, being breathed.

21

The general rules are always to breathe out first, right from the base of the abdomen, pulling it gently in, letting it expel all the breath. Hold it for a short time. Then draw in fresh air, again from the bottom of the abdomen, by just letting the diaphragm expand outwards, so that the abdominal wall is tightly stretched. Hold the breath for a short while, sustaining it firmly, gently pressing it down. Release it, breathing out again slowly and evenly. After another pause, holding the empty lungs, breathe in again.

Breathing in binds and combines, holding the breath helps to make everything go right; breathing out loosens and completes by overcoming all limitations. This is not a technique or gymnastic exercise. It should lead to right living and loving, and like love it should become effortless. There may be times when we need to be a little more conscious of it, so that its rhythmic sequence can always be present and flow out spontaneously all the time, even when asleep.

7

Shoulder my yoke and learn from me.
(Matt. 11:29)

SUFFERING is inevitable in a creation that is still developing. All the time our being and becoming are being created; and in this laborious process of growth we tend to look upon suffering as a formidable mystery that conflicts sharply with our human way of thinking. As a result we are often in revolt, but in our heart of hearts we know God can never be the cause of our suffering. Our Lord suffered torments of anguish of mind and body in the Garden of Gethsemane because he felt he had been abandoned, even by his Father. Yet he suffered because of his love for us. Only those who love suffer. Christ died and shed his blood for us all, so that we could share his love. We cannot compare our own sufferings to those of Christ, but as we follow him we will find his love always sustains.

All through life we have to strive for the human and for what is necessary for life; it is not spoonfed to us. Yet at the same time the spiritual should accompany it and rise from it. All through life too we have to learn to accept our age and the limitations it brings. It is only then that Christ can assume any growth in our lives. We should always pray to him for the passion for living, especially at middle life. This seems to be the most critical period in life. There comes at this time for both men and women a climacteric, a change of life, that affects them physically, psychologically and spiritually. As they approach it they do need a sense of peace and security. It is a time that is marked by a general slowing down. The danger for most people is that they are so wrapped up in daily work, that they have little time for introspection to examine the changes that are taking place. As a result they feel off colour and are led to taking stimulants, drugs, alcohol and tobacco, not so much for pleasure, but through a vague desire to recover diminishing energy. With this goes the temptation to self-righteousness, to rigidity and obstinacy, that are simply defence mechanisms dictated by the unconscious.

Really, middle life can be a time that is most satisfying and fruitful. Dr. Jung insisted that it was a time for the unfolding of the Self, what he called the Illumination of the Self. It should be a time of greater interior life, spiritually and psychologically, when we begin to find within ourselves all we previously projected and sought outside. Christ is still our life, and we should try to be more conscious of his presence, remembering St. Paul's words: 'Anyone who is joined to the Lord is one spirit with him' (1 Cor. 6:17). There is still so much to achieve and live for.

Time is dynamic and carries us along, giving rhythm to our lives, and like Christ we have to submit to her enthralments, and wait until eventually the passivities give way to the creative activity of God. All the time he is ahead, beckoning us go forward 'cum omni fiducia' with enthusiasm (Acts 28:31). That is why the future is more beautiful than all the past; we should not be afraid of it. The externals of life go on, they may change, but fullness of being comes from our attachment to Christ, who though remaining in each of us, grows more and more within us. Our living is a process of love. And 'if we live by the truth and in love' as St. Paul says, 'we shall grow in all ways into

Christ' (Eph. 4:15). Christ's own love was a surrender, a surrender to each one of us. He is still at the heart of our living and loving. His hands are always there to mould and create, those hands through which so great a love is transmitted. It is in love too and suffering that those hands are felt. Not one of the smallest fragments of love can ever be lost in him.

8

He has passed from death to life.
(John 5:24)

BEETHOVEN composed a piano sonata that was to be called 'The Appasionata'. There is so much impassion in our lives. To feel intensely involves a very intimate vision of what is experienced. A great part of my life has been dedicated to passivity, a passivity that was not just emptiness, but a passivity that has always been the bearer, as it should, of new life. Passivity in its highest form is the living experience of God, as it were, enfolding and penetrating us; something like what our Blessed Lady experienced during her 'fiat' at the Annunciation. Passivity surrendered to the grace forming hand of God, becomes energized into the highest form of activity.

To have experienced this is to have had an insight into the Paschal Mystery of Death and Resurrection, a mystery that pervades not only our spiritual lives, but also the whole of creation. New life comes only by way of death. This too is to have understood a little of the great mystery of death, and is a preparation for our own death.

In our journey through life to God, only a few walk with us and remain close to our hearts. Circumstances throw us together. In the past I came into close contact with a personality of genius, who had the greatest insight of anyone of his time into the art of Gregorian Chant, for he had surrendered himself completely to it, as a means of experiencing the deep reality of God. That man was the late Dom Jean Desroquette O.S.B. Monk and Priest of Quarr Abbey. I can still hear his intonation of 'Requiem' the opening neume of the Mass for the Dead, an intonation that has all the elements of a Beethoven chord, with its upsurge and then total surrender. Long before the Second Vatican Council he led me into the beauty of the chant of the age old Requiem Mass full, not of morbidity and sadness, but charged with the living energy of Christ's Resurrection, illuminated with light, 'lux perpetua luceat eis'. A reason for introducing the Paschal Candle into our Funeral Rites.

There can be no replacement in our lives for those we love. Love lives in the depths, where each one is uniquely and irreplaceably himself. Our dead do take our hearts with them. It is true the dead are so quiet, so utterly passive; no word of theirs reaches our ears. And we ask: does their love have to abandon us to live with God? Yet God too is silent, like the dead; and at the same time we know he is certainly with us, we experience his immanence. If we listen to him in the silence of our hearts, passive to his love, we begin to understand why God and our dead are so silent. God's silence becomes the sphere where our love can produce its act of faith in his love. God veils his love in silence, so that our love can reveal itself in faith. He seems to forsake us, so that we can find him.

Our dead imitate his silence. It is through silence they speak to us. They are near to us through the audible words of love. Though they are hidden from our eyes, their love reaches out to us from the boundlessness of God's presence and love. It is we who live a dying life. They know no death. It is precisely because of this that they live for us and are with us. They are indeed present to us in the light of Christ's Resurrection. 'Why are you troubled, and why do questionings rise in your hearts?', said the Risen Christ. 'See my hands and my feet, that it is I myself; handle me and see' (Luke 24:38–39). Through our own vision, and in the silence and passivity of our hearts, we can listen to and understand the soundless words of their love. There in our own silence we will learn that the greatest message of our dead is to summon us into the energy and force of Christ's risen life. This we do when we commemorate them in the Liturgy of the Mass: 'Remember, Lord, those who have died and have gone before us, marked with the sign of faith'.

PART TWO

LOVING – A FEMININE MYSTERY

1

May they all be one.
(John 17:21)

ST. PAUL loves to remind us that the world was formed
and finds its fulfilment 'in Christ'. What is given to us
does not take away from God; so that in our growth, in our
living and loving, we are called to the dignity of co-creators
with God. It is true only the grace of God makes divine,
but we can create something capable of becoming divine,
when we act, consciously or unconsciously, under the hand
of God. Through Christ's historic Incarnation the Transcendent became immanent; and by virtue of his Resurrection Christ became King of the universe, and henceforth
his assimilative power is exercised in the formation of his
mystical body. St. Paul told the Philippians, his most
favoured converts: 'He will transfigure these wretched
bodies of ours into copies of his glorious body. He will do
that by the same power with which he can subdue the whole
universe' (Phil. 3:21).

Christ's Resurrection gives him the place of sovereign
dominance as the centre of the universe, into which all
things are gathered. 'It was God's good pleasure to let all
completeness dwell in him' (Col. 1:19), but the universal
powers of Christ operate only by virtue of his Incarnation,

31

and this great mystery of Christianity entered the world, not by virtue of the masculine, but of the feminine soul. The passive element of surrender is an expression of the feminine. Mary by her 'fiat' brought forth Christ and made him known to the world. God chose her to set her above the world, for the child born of her was to be greater than the world.

At certain times of the year, in the early hours of the morning, it is possible to see the sun shining gloriously in the east, but low down as it has not long risen, and also the moon still visible high up in the west, and I love to think of that work of God the 'mysterium coniunctionis', the mysterious union of opposites, man and woman – Christ 'like the sun shining with all its force' (Rev. 1:16) and Mary 'with the moon under her feet' (Rev. 12:1). It is true Mary's powers flow not from any inner necessity, but only from the divine pleasure. Likewise it is true the fullness of the world lies in Christ, Christ God and Man, who by virtue of the Incarnation, crowned by the Resurrection became the centre of creation. St. Paul sums it up in his Letter to the Colossians with the words: 'in ipso omnia constant'. Christ 'holds all things in unity' (Col. 1:17), but in his plan for this oneness of creation, it was the feminine soul that was chosen to help form the whole Christ. Christ was consecrated through Mary for this cosmic function. Mary and the Church too in their nature and vocation in the pattern of the feminine are identical, both present Christ to us to lead us to wholeness and sanctity. It is the feminine that draws out all that is best in us. Mary, in whom the feminine is so beautifully presented, symbolizes the force of surrender of all creation. In her the whole of creation becomes the sanctuary of God. In Mary's passivities we, both men and women, learn to recognize our feminine soul and passivities, and allow ourselves to be energized and activated, as she did, by the Spirit of God (Luke 1:35).

There is a sum total that makes up our life, what the late Dr. Jung called a Process of Individuation. By that is meant a gentle process that enables us to find a wholeness and maturity within ourselves. The 'mysterium coniunctionis' is something very intimate to the oneness of us all. It is simply the integration, the linking within ourselves, of all the polar complementary components of our being, masculine and feminine, conscious and unconscious, activities and passivities in a living relationship. We develop by way of an energy that is psychic; consciousness emerges from the womb of the unconscious. We advance through a 'libido', that is an energy, that regresses and progresses in what is termed an Individuation Process, the confrontation of the polar complementary forces of opposites within ourselves. This Individuation Process is concerned with the interior of our own inner cosmos; for this man needs the help of his feminine soul and woman her masculine soul. Long before physiologists demonstrated that by reason of our glandular structure there are both male and female elements in all of us, men and women, it was said that every man carries a woman within himself and every woman a man. In his work for Individuation a man has to strive to penetrate the hymen of his archetypal woman, something most deep and precious to him, something that alone can make him a complete whole person. It is something no one else can pierce or take possession of; that is why Jung called her Anima, the soul of man, soul used not in the Scholastic sense, but as part of a man's living personality. Likewise for woman he used the term Animus for her masculine soul.

Jung showed how the Anima has a truly salvific role to play in guiding a man to maturity. It is through her that he enters into his unconscious. It is she who brings his Shadow qualities to light with all their dark traits of immaturity. When repressed or neglected, when women in general are treated with contempt, her dark side of seductress manifests herself by way of moods, in fantasies and emotional outbursts. It is she who makes a man jealous and critical, creates vague and unpleasant sensations in him, persuades him he is sick, and haunts his sleep life with seductive dreams. In his Gospel St. Matthew tells us Our Lord entered an official's house, took his daughter by the hand and raised her up. 'The little girl is not dead, she is asleep' (Matt. 9:24). It is only what is unconscious in our lives that can harm us. When the Anima is accepted and embraced, brought to a conscious level, her power to harm is lessened. In her positive role she is the capacity for all the artistic gifts of man and all the wonderful beauty of his creative mind. Indeed, the image of the feminine is reflected in all the creative work of man. Likewise the Anima is the capacity for every sort of affectionate and loving relationship and prepares a man for his experience of the woman in the world outside.

Man and woman by themselves risk sterility in their individual lives because of narrowness and onesidedness. The masculine element in man does not suffice, nor does the feminine in woman. In a true sense the Anima and the Animus are the contrasexual partners of man and woman. To have seen this and to have accepted this relationship and to have made a complete surrender to it in an 'hierosgamos', in a sacred marriage, within the Self, in a relationship that is real, living and loving, is the basis for maturity and oneness.

The Risen Christ is the Centre of all centres, and any unity we may achieve is nothing if it is not born of Christ. 'He holds all things in unity' (Col. 1:17); he is all one, and he does come down into the work of his creation to consolidate its unification. The more concerned we are in forming this unity, the more God will flood into it his own irresistible simplicity. Individuation is for Jung an in – dividual process, a process by which we become separate indivisible beings. This union is achieved by the conscious confrontation of opposites and their synthesis within ourselves. God acts upon our whole being by the infusion of grace, so much so that Jung saw the archetype of the formation of the Self, which results from this union, as the 'Imago Dei', the Image of God. I like to view this formation of the Self in the light of Pauline theology. In experiencing the symbolic contents of our human psyche we encounter principles that strengthen our belief in and our love for God. St. Paul has the same idea of the Self in his letters to the Colossians and Ephesians; and it is good that the Jerusalem Bible keeps the Knox version of rendering 'the new self' progressing and being renewed 'in the image of its creator' (Col. 3:10 and Eph. 4:24). The tension that results from this union of opposites is an energy that is ever recreative, a renewing evolutively and involutively 'until we become the perfect Man, fully mature with the fulness of Christ himself' (Eph. 4:13). In this passage of St. Paul the Jerusalem Bible refers the 'Man' to Christ, the archetype of all who are reborn. The Self here of course has nothing in common with the godlikeness of the superman and his inflated Ego and ego-centredness. The Self is the centre of the personality, which encloses the whole of our being.

The person who is whole and mature is an individual, but not an individualist. The Individuation process could never make us selfish, rather it should help fulfil our individual natures; for in being true to ourselves we are in the best relationship to Christ and to everything else. That is why in 'Hamlet' Polonius' last words to his son Laertes were: 'This above all; to thine own self be true, and it must follow, as night the day thou canst not then be false to any man'. The Individuation Process makes us aware of our own unique natures, of our relationship to Christ and to all life, human, animal and plant. It personalizes, makes us persons, and at the same time totalizes us; for the wholeness we achieve within becomes a contact with the Person of Christ and his work of communion and mission in the life of the Church. It brings that experience of oneness, the desire of Our Lord that 'they all be one' (John 17:21). It reconciles us with life, which can now be accepted as it is, and not as we would like it to be. It was this that fascinated St. Francis, and St. Paul too assured the Colossians: 'There is only Christ: he is everything and he is in everything' (Col. 3:11). He then goes on to list the fruits of Individuation: 'He loves you, and you should be clothed in sincere compassion, in kindness and humility, gentleness and patience. Bear with one another; forgive each other as soon as a quarrel begins. The Lord has forgiven you; you must do the same. Over all these clothes, to keep them together and complete them, put on love. And may the peace of Christ reign in your hearts, because it is for this that you were called together as parts of one body' (Col. 3:12–15).

It is a fact that all flesh is weak but it does rise again with Christ to form a new earth, what St. Paul calls 'the body of Christ'. Indeed, he says there is only one process in formation, that of the building up of the body of Christ. 'All of us, in union with Christ, form one body, and as parts of it we belong to each other' (Rom. 12:5). He saw so clearly that history resolves itself in a synthesis, that through this process and through the lives of countless people one single operation is progressing – the growth of Christ, the Christ who is everywhere present, the Christ who was consecrated to be the force and moulding principle of the universe (Col. 1:15–20). It is put so beautifully in his letter to the Ephesians: 'He has put all things under his feet, and made him, as ruler of everything, the head of the Church; which is his body, the fullness of him who fills the whole of creation' (Eph. 1:22–23).

In its widest sense St. Paul includes in his concept of the body of Christ the entire world as unified under 'the Lord Christ', but adds: 'the body grows until it has built itself up, in love' (Eph. 4:16). The world is held together not by matter but by spirit, and love is the one spirit, as Our Lord said, that gives life (John 6:63). God alone is transcendent, the source and creator of life, the object of love at the summit of the world, the supreme force that attracts all growth. But it was through the Incarnation of his Son that his love became visible and tangible in the world of his creation (John 1:4,9). Christ became the living centre, the point of convergence, who draws to himself all the innumerable personal energies of every age (Eph. 1:10,22), so that a single body and soul emerges from the world, the Christ who said he would draw the whole of creation to himself (John 12:32). The single energy that draws all things to Christ and draws him to us, is the energy of love (1 John 4:7–16). Indeed love is the most universal and mysterious of all energies. As we grow an energy should emerge within our integrated Self, in which love becomes the highest form of our consciousness. Just as we can trace the presence of energy from its rudimentary level to its powerful radiation in ourselves, so too to be certain of love within ourselves we should assume its presence, at least in an inchoate form, in everthing that is. 'God is love' (1 John 4:16), and he plants it in all his creation.

Love is a single passion that springs up in the hearts of us all; without it the world would dry up and wither. In all of us love is an energy that is ever recreative. Only love brings us to completion, because it is only love that takes possession of us and unites us by what lies deepest within us. If the spirit of God's earth is to be born within us, we must experience the mystery of love. 'This is what the Lord asks of you', proclaimed the prophet Micah, 'only this, to act justly, to love tenderly, and to walk humbly with your God' (Micah 6:8). Today this divine request is sadly neglected. The world has lost the great art of living and loving.

In this life we can in the limits of our creatureliness perceive God in creation. He does communicate himself to our human hearts in the subjective experience of knowledge and love. Passivity was the first reality God created, a passivity of 'a formless void' (Gen. 1:2), open to his creating hand; that is why all creation is created as it were as openness to God. For fruitfulness he needs the feminine, the passivity and receptivity of our creaturely nature. In a real sense the whole of creation stands before God as feminine, and each of us, man and woman, is like Mary a 'Theotokos', the feminine bearer of God. Love too in its last analysis is a feminine not a masculine mystery.

Today when man has lost contact with his unconscious, and so with his feminine soul, and woman in her desire for equality rejects her own femininity, so few really know how to love. Jung too said love was a feminine mystery, and he maintained that psychologically the opposite to love is not hate, but the will to power. Where love and the feminine mystery are missing the will to power predominates, as also where the will to power is paramount love is missing. This is very evident in the aggression of our age, and can be seen in wars, violence and terrorism, riots and the lack of all restraint. The remedy can be found in our acceptance of the feminine. That is why a man must start 'in the beginning' with his relationship to the archetypal Eve.

Life is born of the spark of opposites; there is no energy without the tension of opposites (Sirach 42:24). Consciousness, even without being aware of it, seeks its unconscious opposite. It is only what is unconscious that can harm us, and everything unconscious is always projected. As long as the Anima is unconscious she will always be projected on women in general. When women are made up, as they usually are, to be erotically desirable, it is so easy for the immature man to project his Anima on anyone who comes along. Such love affairs are psychologically soulless. Whereas when the man, who is sufficiently whole as to be aware of his Anima, sees her reflected in the flesh, he knows that this woman is She. He feels he has known her intimately for all time, that his whole life has been a preparation for this encounter. She is recognized as the bearer of his own 'soul image'. Presented with the reality of her being, his inner feminine soul is stimulated to action, and his power to love becomes positive and creative. The process is the same for a woman and her Animus, her masculine soul.

In this way a man and woman know intuitively that each is the bearer of the 'soul image' of the other; they come into complete possession of themselves and become lost in one another. They become united by what lies deepest within them and can approach each other in perfect freedom; their whole being is lifted up through the transforming power of the Self. They can go out to each other without any lust for possession, for they both know that they already possess within what each of them seeks without. Surrender then becomes a revelation, it is a gift of oneself. Every night the earth dissipates its energy to love, because the object of its love is only partially understood.

When a man and woman are sufficiently whole and individuated they stand before each other as the attraction and symbol, not only of their own feminine and masculine souls, but also of the whole universe. In their relationship Christ has the first place, since as St Paul says he fills the whole of creation with his presence (Eph. 4:10 and 1 Cor. 12:6). As they rescue each other from loneliness, they become alive to their true function and discover a new energy. Not only does each become the bearer of the 'soul image' to the other, but also in the fullness of the Self the bearer of the 'God image' as well. Each communicates God to the other. Each is the earthly vessel in which the divine experience is carried, and this image with the help of grace can become brighter and brighter as each reflects it to the other (2 Cor. 3:18). In this way man and woman become the creators of each other. In a special way a woman leads a man to God, for the holier she is the more she is woman, and in his deep love for her, like Dante, he sees her eyes resting on God.

In the Gospel story St. Luke tells us that Christ was not afraid to let a woman touch him, and adds that at her touch

Christ 'felt that power had gone out from' him (Luke 8:43–48); her faith in Man had power to make her whole. We cannot live on earth without experiencing the emotional level, we cannot deny our feelings. But if we love Christ, his Spirit will direct our love, not only our spiritual but also our physical love; and here on earth can we separate them? The within and the without, the radial and the tangential exist together. Matter is tangential, something that classifies and separates, and because of this divides and finally disintegrates. It is the radial, something within, spirit, something that has the being of oneness in all that is and which must eventually converge on the All, that holds all things together (Eph. 4:6 and Col. 1:17). That is why the radial is the spirit of love that Our Lord said is the spirit of life (John 6:63). The world feels for the tangential because it can touch it, but then must finally lose it. It is the radial that gives real meaning to love, a love that can never be lost, but must continually grow and deepen.

Love has a power to find its way to certainty, for 'in Christ' everything finds its fulfilment. In our striving for wholeness and Individuation, whether we be celibate or married, we do experience the presence of God. God reveals himself in love, and this love is 'made visible in Christ Jesus our Lord' (Rom. 8:39). Christ's image is implanted in each one of us by the Spirit of God himself. 'You are a letter from Christ, drawn up by us, and written not with ink but with the Spirit of the living God, not on stone tablets but on the tablets of your living hearts' (2 Cor. 3:3). The true image of God in us, disfigured by sin, was restored by Christ, so that in the totality of the Self a new Self 'is renewed in the image of its creator' (Col. 3:10). We are always stirred by what already exists in us. By way of our inner polarity we find our totality; and in so doing it is inevitable that we should experience the image of the Christ we carry within and see reflected without. The stronger this image is, the stronger will be the spirit of love. St. John says that such a love is not just mere words and talk, but something real and active

(1 John 3:18). It is constituted by the living presence of Christ, and the paradox is 'as long as we love one another God will live in us' (1 John 4:12). To have seen this is a treasure, for this mutual ability of ours to love is simply two phases of a single movement. Christ is the binding force behind it, and since 'he is your life' (Col. 3:4), united with him a sense of oneness and togetherness is formed. Formed 'in Christ', such a love is timeless and spaceless, for it is the infinite, transcending as it does man and woman, that makes it possible to have an eternal love.

Christ's assumption of flesh unites him immanently to the whole of creation at every level, past, present and to come, as a living centre to which all love and affinity converge. And for this, can we not say he depends on the feminine mystery of love? St. Paul told the Colossians: 'There is only Christ: he is everything and is in everything' (Col. 3:11). Christ is the one centre of the universe, and his presence radiates from the within, in the heart of all that is. It is the within in everything that has the same essence of oneness. By way of all that lies deep within us we come into the most complete possession of ourselves. We become one, and yet at the same time, the one becomes aligned to the many – one with the Self and one with the world. Everything seeks fulfilment, and all that is beautiful finds its completion. Our Lord put it this way in his prayer to his Father: 'I have given them the glory you gave to me, that they may be one as we are one. With me in them and you in me, may they be so completely one that the world will realise that it was you who sent me and that I have loved them as much as you loved me' (John 17:22–23).

2

Happy are your eyes because they see.
(Matt. 13:16)

IT WAS upon St. Bernadette at Lourdes that Our
Blessed Lady smiled, to whom she made herself known
with the words: 'I am the Immaculate Conception'.
Another Frenchman, who had a deep love for Our Lady,
Fr. Teilhard de Chardin, loved to call her feast day of
December 8th 'the feast of passive action'. Indeed, in Our
Lady's spotlessness we have the source of all action.
Through her Immaculate Conception Mary was made the
instrument of God, adorned to become the Mother of God.

Purity is essentially an active virtue, because it concentrates
God in us; it draws God to us, to be radiated to all those
with whom we come into contact. Our Lady was conceived
and born in the most perfect state of grace, of perfect
passivity, which is at the same time perfect action. The
work of God was so active in her, that all the activity of her
life would never lessen nor destroy it.

The psychology of Dr. Jung can be used in a truly
Christian way. Using his terminology, could we not say
that this grace helped to make Mary the complete woman,
from whom the Individualized Self emerged with a
wholeness and maturity that no other woman had or can

ever attain? From this too emerged her masculine activities of courage, objectivity, and spiritual wisdom – the positive Animus that has helped stimulate men all down the centuries, and must irresistibly have drawn St. Joseph to her. What a difference from Eve, the natural mother, whose face, so full of mystery, is lost in the distant past.

One year on December 7th. a great and dear friend, a convert Jew, wrote to greet me: 'Tomorrow God's partner, the Great Mother, will be "the air we breathe" – "wild air, world mothering air, nestling me everywhere" '. In his great epic 'The Divine Comedy' when Dante finally enters heaven, it is St. Bernard, 'the Mellifluous Doctor', who leads him to the vision of Christ. St. Bernard bids him first look higher to the face of Mary, the enthroned Queen. Hers is the face most like unto the face of Christ, and its brilliance alone can make us fit to see Christ.

3

To entertain the very thought of her is maturity of mind.
(Wisdom 6:15)

ALL TRUE Christian piety must also be piety to Our Blessed Lady. It is in the light of Mary that the Church sees herself as Mother and the Spotless Bride of Christ. That is why the Church, in the recent decree on herself 'De Ecclesia' at the Second Vatican Council, finds it impossible to speak of her role in salvation history without referring to Mary. Pope Paul VI too in his Apostolic Exhortation, 'Marialis Cultus', writing to his fellow Bishops, expressed his hope that there will be among the clergy and people entrusted to their care a salutary increase of devotion to Mary with undoubted profit for the Church and society.

For some years I have had the privilege of living and working in Corby. It is true that for the most part the community has its roots in Scotland and Ireland, yet the love the town has for Our Lady is something very Christian, and does enhance the deep love this country always had for Mary. Corby is at the heart of a living tradition.

Right from early days, St. Athanasius and St. Hilary testify to the support the British Bishops gave at the Council of Sardica A.D. 343 to the orthodox teaching of the divinity and humanity of Christ, from which all true devotion to Our Lady comes. Not only is the name of Mary found and revered and praised in the poetry of the Welsh Bards, under the influence of St. Cadoc and Dewi Sant (St. David), but also on the other side of the border in Britain too the name of Mary shines as a beacon to the rest of the Western Church. St Bede tells us in his homily 'On the Purification' that the Saxons looked with special devotion on the most Blessed Mother of God. The Saxons too had their poets, Caedmon, Aldhelm, Bede, Alcuin, Ethelwolf, and Wolston, but for the most part their verses on Our Lady have been handed down to us in Latin, all in classical metre. It was the Saxon Monk Alcuin who, in the distribution of the various Offices of the week, assigned Saturday to Our Lady; and whom in all probability composed and put together the beautiful Saturday Mass 'Salve Sancta Parens' in her honour.

It is well to remind ourselves from time to time of the debt of gratitude we owe to the wonderful Monastic tradition that helped spread the faith in this country. First the Monastic system of the Celts, with its missionary and educational activity, which had its origin in the Latin culture of Gallic Monasticism, started this tradition. Men like Cadoc, Dyfrig, Illtyd and David in Wales, Colmcille, Columbanus and Ninian in Scotland, and later under the Benedictine influence Wilfrid, Benedict Biscop, Willibrord, Bede, Boniface, and Aldhelm in England spread the faith and preserved for posterity the beauty of their tradition and their love for Our Lady. Long before the Norman Invasion there is more than abundant evidence in this Island of a true devotion to Our Lady, based on the belief in her divine maternity.

There are still in this country so many beautiful relics of a love for Our Lady. From the noonday Angelus, Saturday was a public holiday in her honour. Flowers were called after her as symbols of her virtues – the lily of purity, the

45

rose of love, the violet of humility and so on. Individual flowers bore her name. The snowdrop was called 'the fair maid of February', the lungwort when it was in flower for her Annunciation 'Our Lady's milk wort', many varieties of clematis were called 'the Virgin's bower' because they came into flower at her Visitation, were in full bloom for her Assumption and faded at her Nativity. Honeysuckle was 'Our Lady's fingers', cowslip 'Our Lady's keys', periwinkle 'The Virgin's flower' and fuchsia 'Our Lady's eardrops'. Even today a few bear her name – the marigold, ladysmock, lady's seal, and there is a variety of thistle with its white milk known as 'Carduus Marianus'.

There are many other signs of national and popular devotion to Mary. Towns were called after her, altars and bells dedicated to her, ships were named after her, alms, 'Our Lady's loaf ', were given in love of her, soldiers carried her image on their shields. From this devotion a love for her Divine Son sprang up, and a chivalrous respect for the fair sex. A new type of character, so sadly missing today, arose in the person of the Virgin Mother, and a moral charm and beauty of female excellence was felt. An old poem ran: 'To unpraise a woman it were a shame, for a woman was thy dame'.

Mary is at the heart of our living and loving. In his recent Encyclical Letter 'The Mother of the Redeemer' Pope John Paul II places Our Lady at the centre of 'the pilgrim Church'. It was through her that the light of this world came to birth. That is why tradition has it: 'To love the Mother is to honour her Son', and is a mark of predestination. Each of us has to allow the creative work of God to be completed in our lives; and in this Mary is our guide. Mary is like the voice of the universe looking forward to completion. At her Annunciation she willed and accepted the breath of the Holy Spirit, conceived and brought forth. Something like this has to go on in our lives all the time, the ability to be receptive, to allow the creative work of God to go on and advance. The 'Hail Mary' portrays the eternal reality of the Annunciation within us. It brings the conviction that life and love spring up, always and everywhere, within us and around us, and all we have to do is to say with Mary 'fiat', thy will be done, and mean it. Things happen to us, but when we make our surrender, God does infuse into us the creative energy of his love. 'And the grace of our Lord filled me with faith and with the love that is in Christ Jesus' (1 Tim. 1:14).

4

From that moment the disciple made a place for her in his home.
(John 19:27)

TODAY most people are conscious of their changed relationship with nature. Primitive people held that in the last analysis all problems were human problems. For according to them the way Mother Nature behaved depended on whether their actions were pleasing or displeasing to the Gods. In days gone by our ancestors were helpless before the forces of nature; they were her slaves. With the advance of science and technology the roles have changed. Today if we are not the complete masters, we at least treat her as a partner.

With the advance in knowledge there is a danger of losing respect for what was once held in awe. As dogma too develops there may be a tendency to forget what was once treasured, to forget that our advance in the cone of space-time rests on a basis of deep culture that must never be destroyed. In recent years there have been some who seem to despise Mariology, to look upon it as sentimental and an obstacle to the advance of ecumenism. Even at the recent Vatican Council the atmosphere became explosive when the Marian question was approached. The question whether or not Our Lady should find a place in the Schema on the Church, voted on October 29th. 1963, developed into a melodrama. Many Fathers wanted a separate document on Our Lady, but eventually it was decided to devote the last chapter to her in the 'Constitution on the Church', to link her more closely with the main theme of the Council.

We advance through time. Time is dynamic. Yet through all time there must run a continuity and kinship, even in our devotions. There can be no such thing as a cessation. Everything that happens is a meaningful chain in the episodes of life, an 'aurora consurgens', like Mary herself, a dawning that rises out of the mists of antiquity, stretching out to the light of what is still to come. It is good to see that in the decree 'De Ecclesia' on herself, the Church encourages us 'in the cult of the Virgin Mary' and asks her theologians and preachers to be careful in their considerations of the Mother of God's unique dignity, to refrain from falsehood by way of superlatives, as also from a narrow-mindedness. She tells us that the outstanding grace of Mary's role as Mother of God makes her outstrip by far all other creatures in excellence, whether they are in heaven or on earth. Yet at the same time she is not above creatures; she is still linked 'to all men in need of salvation'. She is 'a wholly unique member of the Church'.

It is in the light of Mary that we too come to see ourselves as individuals. Light in this world is followed by shadow. To deny the presence of evil would be to turn from reality. Evil is a veritable power. The world is shaken by shudders and dark forebodings, by the lust for power, by political situations and the arms race. The question posed by the Gnostics of old is asked today: whence comes evil? They looked for a principle outside of themselves; the root cause is surely within. So few people today experience the divine image as the innermost possession of their souls. Christ only meets them from without, never from within the soul; that is why a dark paganism reigns there. The religious archetype is so dynamic, it must find an expression in conscious activity and growth. When it is denied its lawful expression in the true worship of God it finds an external outlet in the ideals of collective identities, in forms of socialism and philanthropic activity. It can also be fretted away in the occult and superstitious; it finds perversions in the social evils of drink, sex and drugs. In religion too it can find an outlet in ritualistic observance, in a dogmatism and morality that lack a true inner meaning.

If we wish to have an answer to the problems of our day we need first and foremost a self-knowledge of our own wholeness. We must know to what heights we can ascend and the depths of crimes we are capable of. We must beware of looking at the first as real and the other as a mere illusion. Both are living elements within us and both are bound to come to light, should we wish to live without self-delusion. This calls for a profound insight into ourselves. We know that something alien in us does come our way, just as an inspiration or dream emerges of its own accord. We are handicapped by our own weakness and by what still lies hidden within us. Things happen to us and it is only by great effort that we succeed in conquering and establishing for ourselves an area of freedom. When we have won this achievement, we can confront our inner reality, a numen if you like, a mysterious part of us that we cannot make disappear, however much we would like. Jacob wrestled with an angel and came away lame, and his story was accepted without question. He called the name of the place Peniel 'because I have seen God face to face' (Gen. 32:30). Today he would be laughed at and jeered. Yet how true this is of all of us. In each of us there is an inner conflict, and conflict always presupposes a higher sense of responsibility. There is an inner court where we must pass judgement on ourselves and meet the true Self 'created in God's way' (Eph. 4:24). It is disunity within ourselves that causes us to identify ourselves with our surroundings. Jung pointed out the danger today of looking outwards to collective ideologies, of blaming our faults on others, of trying to force laws on others and of even trying to destroy the existing order of things. But the great problems of humanity are never solved by laws and exterior force; they are solved by a regeneration of the attitudes of individuals. An inner revolution and renewal is required if we are to advance.

Each of us, like Mary herself, feels the need to set our feet on the road that ascends. And yet, as the feast of her Assumption implies, the paradox is that we ascend by descending, or rather ascent and descent, progression and regression are two phases of a single movement of growth. They are the normal states of a healthy life. True there is no way back to the original innocence of Eden. Nevertheless, we do feel the need for immersion and emergence. Our Lord put it this way: 'Unless one is born anew, he cannot see the kingdom of God' (John 3:3). The Church today, to use her own words at the Second Vatican Council, 'has deliberate intention of throwing light on .the Blessed Virgin's function in the mystery of the Word made flesh and the Mystical Body, and on the duties of men, who have been redeemed, towards the Mother of God, Mother of Christ and Mother of men' (De Ecclesia). Mary is the Mother of us all. It is in her womb that we are to be renewed. This is to speak in symbols, but the symbol and the image are not the irresponsible creation of our souls; rather they respond to a need and fulfil a function of bringing to light the most hidden modalities of being. Mary is the Great Mother. It is in the secret of her dark womb that we enter to emerge again to the light of day with a much deeper knowledge of ourselves and our own position in the mystery of the Church. St. Paul says the Lord 'will bring to light the things now hidden in darkness and will disclose the purposes of the heart' (1 Cor. 4:5). This is not to give expression to incestuous desires, rather it is the lawful need to return to the source from which all creative life and love spring.

'Mary has made an entry in depth into the history of salvation. She gathers in herself the greatest resolutions of faith and sets them reverberating' (De Ecclesia). Mary like us is a creature, though without stain or wrinkle. Mary is a mother and yet a maid. Mary kept her secret, pondering it in her heart, and for this she was made whole (Luke 2:52). Because of this, Mary's motherhood 'in the economy of grace has no pause in its duration from the consent she loyally gave at the Annunciation, until the everlasting consummation of all the elect... Raised into heaven she has not laid aside this saving office, but she persists, with many pleas, in winning us the gifts of salvation' (De Ecclesia). This maternal duty of Mary towards us in no way diminishes the unique mediation of Christ, her Son. Christ is Lord of Lords and the Conqueror of sin and death. Mary's powers flow from God's good pleasure; her beatitude comes not from action, but from the passivity of what matured in her womb.

Because the Church is human she exists in time and is subject to the forces of history; because she is divine she is aided by grace in an ever forward movement. Weak and sinful, we feel the constant need for purification; it is Mary, as Mother of the Church, who leads us on to renewal. She is, as the 'Constitution on the Church' says, 'a Mother to us in the order of grace... Taken up to heaven, she did not lay aside this saving role, but by her manifold acts of intercession continues to win for us gifts of salvation'. It is fitting that she, who by the divine pleasure was to be the Great Mother, should not only be preserved from the attraction and allurements of the perfume of Mother Earth and what matures in her breast, but should also escape from being swallowed up in the womb of Mother Earth, and thus be taken up, body and soul, into heavenly glory upon the completion of her earthly sojourn. The Assumption of Mary into heaven is the fulfilling in advance of what is promised to the pilgrim Church. Indeed, as long as there is a single soul on earth Mary will continue as a symbol and sign. In her all is done that with us is still to come. That is why the Church, in the closing words of the decree on herself, says: 'In the bodily and spiritual glory which she possesses in heaven, the Mother of Jesus continues in this present world as the image and first flowering of the Church as she is to be perfected in the world to come. Likewise, Mary shines forth on earth, until the Lord shall come, as a sign of sure hope and solace for the pilgrim People of God' (De Ecclesia).

5

This mystery has many implications.
(Eph. 5:32)

IN RECENT YEARS much has been made of the term the 'Eternal Feminine', but Paul Claudel used it as early as 1909 to describe the role of the Church, as well as that of Our Lady. He looked upon woman as someone on whose forehead the word 'mystery' is inscribed, and spoke about 'the woman who is the Church'. He had a great love for the Church and called her the Great Mother, upon whose knees he learnt all he knew. The Church is the Sacrament of Christ in history, the Mother who brings to birth the children of God. Indeed, history is, as St. Paul reminds us, the bringing to birth of a divine reality (Rom. 8:22–23). It is the Church in history that continues the mission of Christ, and is animated by his Spirit, working at the same task as her Master – making men and women holy. It is in Mother Church that we begin to find a communion with each other. 'All grow into one holy temple in the Lord' (Eph. 2:21).

We all possess a fine flair for the spirit of our age. In an age that seeks to know, and draws us into the vastness of the universe, it is religion that binds us to the ground of the sacred. It is religion, with its hold on symbols, that preserves eternal truths within us. Symbols are never invented, they just happen. In an age that seeks to equate faith and reason, in an age of the New Pentecost, symbols preserve in us the need to communicate on the sacred and numinous level. It is symbolism that presents reality to us and preserves in us our person, that which profoundly we are.

The Church, mindful of her role as Mother, honours her buildings with a Solemn Rite of Dedication, and urges her faithful to celebrate the anniversaries with a feast. It is a feast that must always be personal to a particular Parish and its Church; and yet through its symbolism it is a feast that brings with it a deep sense of 'fellowship', the belonging together, that St. Paul had in mind of living and loving (2 Cor. 13:13). Through Christ's presence and through his vivifying action, it is a feast a Parish shares with neighbouring Catholics and Christians and the rest of its Diocese, but also in view of what St. Paul meant by the 'Pleroma' with the rest of the world. To celebrate the anniversary is to bring a little more unity and completion to our world.

The reality which the building symbolizes is more wonderful, more beautiful, certainly more ageless than the actual building itself. If we go back to the early Christian community in Rome, to the time when a consecrated building had not been possible, perhaps not even thought of, to the time when the Church, in the words of St. Paul, met at the house of Prisca and Aquila (1 Cor. 16:19), the word Church was not used to designate a building for worship, but to describe the society of Christians. Yet by fortunate coincidence in our English language we use the same word to describe each, allowing us to reflect, as we are meant to, on the building as a symbol of society. The society of Christians is unparalleled. Unlike other societies that function through the agreement of their members, the Church is kept in being by a union more real than its members. It is a union 'in Christ'. For all the failings of its members, it is at core indestructible, because it is holy. We ought to have a great sense of the holiness of the Church, and today when she is so much under attack, we should have a sufficiently clear sense in what that holiness consists. It is the embodying of an heavenly reality. 'Embodying' is a fitting word, for the Church is the Body of Christ, the fullness and completeness of Christ. It is a fullness and completeness of undeserved generosity. Pope Pius XII in his Encyclical Letter 'Mystici Corporis' spoke about Christ in the Church being brought to complete fulfilment. We can find another expression of this reality in St. Paul. Drawing a parallel with the Jewish Temple, he wrote to the Ephesians: 'You are citizens like all the saints, and part of God's household. You are part of a building that has the apostles and prophets for its foundations, and Christ Jesus himself for its main corner stone. As every structure is aligned on him, all grow into one holy temple in the Lord; and you too, in him, are being built into a house where God lives, in the Spirit' (Eph. 2:19–22).

Not only is the building of a Church symbolical of the whole body of Christians, it also presents us with the truth that each one of us is a temple of God. This is so because of Christ's presence amongst us. St John tells us that Christ pitched his tent amongst us (John 1:14). The Incarnation of the Word of God makes him personally present to us; no longer the presence of the Divine Wisdom enshrined in the Mosaic Law. It is the body of the Risen Christ, the temple that Christ raised up, the spiritual temple from which living waters flow, that is present to us. The author of the letter to the Hebrews does not hesitate to say: 'Christ was faithful as a son, and as the master in the house. And we are his house' (Heb. 3:6).

Just as in the Jewish Temple there was an inner sanctuary, accessible only to the High Priest, so too in the spiritual temple which we make up, there is a sanctuary into which we enter only through Christ. This mystery of temple and sanctuary is symbolized in the building of a Church with its sanctuary and altar. On the day of its solemn dedication the spiritual reality is made ever present. This fact is made even truer by the Real Presence of Christ in the Blessed Sacrament; so that as often as we receive Holy Communion there, we enter with Christ into the heavenly sanctuary as perfectly as is possible in this life. This heavenly and ageless reality is enshrined for us in terms of consecrated stone and mortar, wood and glass, so that we can live in anticipation of the heavenly reality for which we hope. We recall all the Masses offered there, each the sacrificial act of Christ himself, by which he entered the sanctuary as both Priest and Victim to give us his heavenly gifts and to draw us after him. We think of all the baptisms, confirmations, acts of reconciliation, weddings, anointings of the sick, rites of reception into the Church and funerals. It must be with joyful and grateful hearts that we contemplate the many graces and favours we have received in that sanctuary.

It is the eternal that gives meaning to the present, just as with vision and insight and through symbolism the present becomes eternal. So often it is woman who holds the key that opens the way of the future; though it be man's besetting temptation to use her as the key to close the door on the present. It is significant that a Church should always have its shrine to Our Lady to depict her in her role of Woman and Mother. In herself Mary was contained by Christ, because she is his creature; he called her so by the title 'woman'. Yet by her obedience she contained him in her body and heart. He still contains her, for he is God, and he is still contained by her, because she brings him into being in us, conceiving us in his Mystical Body. The building of a Church besides its deliberate likeness to the features of the holy Church of God, with its walls and roof, its sanctuary and altar, has also an unstated and yet undeniable likeness to the Mother of God. Even without a shrine to her, if that were thinkable, a Church would be a place where she would inevitably be found and honoured.

For the human place where Christ still loves to be, is with Mary.

The interior of the building of a Church is symbolical of the fertile womb, from which all life and love flow, free from all abortive influence. As often as we enter there, we emerge in accordance with Christ's injunction reborn to new life (John 3:5–7). There too we find that new life is born from the spark of opposites, not only of man and woman, but also of the human and divine, of action and passion, of the known and the unknown. The great problems of society are connected with the individual, and it is in the spacious womb of the building of a Church that we enter the dark womb of our own being. The way we there solve our own problems will depend to a large extent the future, not only of the Church herself, but also of society.

Our present day world seeks only to relieve the needs of society and improve its living conditions. It does not see the importance of the individual's need for spiritual renewal and psychological growth. To remain true to ourselves we must mount to greater consciousness and love. In doing so we find ourselves joined to all those who are making the same pilgrimage with us, and how numerous they are and how different their ways of life. Love is the one ecumenical hope. Today the Church is more aware of her universal role. The chief emphasis of the recent Vatican Council has been a reawakening of the Church's mission of love, not only to her own members, but to all Christian bodies and to all men and women. All go to form the body of Christ. This body is only kept in being by a spirit of love, which gives joy to all living. 'I have told you this so that my own joy may be in you and your joy be complete' (John 15:11).

PART THREE

LOVING AND PRAYING

1

Lord, teach us to pray.
(Luke 11:1)

THE JOY of living and loving makes us sensitive to our
need to be open to God in prayer. Indeed, the art of
prayer is the secret of all living and loving; but to grasp its
art something more than words is necessary. It takes
personal experience, which the Spirit of Jesus alone can
give. Even the words falling from Our Lord's own lips were
not enough to complete the disciples' apprenticeship in
prayer. After three years of living and loving with the
Master of prayer, the best among them could not watch
even for an hour. 'The spirit is willing enough, but the flesh
is weak' (Matt. 26:41). We too have been called by Jesus,
and must keep that before our eyes. No human teaching can
do more than Jesus' own words.

Jesus was and always will be the Master of prayer because
he prayed better than anyone before or after him. Jesus
lived the life of perfect prayer, and that in the midst of a life
harassing and sometimes over-powering. But the most
important reason why he is our Master of prayer is because
he alone can place in our minds and hearts the true spirit of
prayer, that of gratuitous love, and that comes from living
with him. We cannot pray until Christ has taught us from
within.

In the Gospel each time Our Lord wished to go off with his disciples to pray, we are told they went to sleep. On Mount Tabor while Jesus was conversing with Moses and Elijah, 'Peter and his companions were heavy with sleep' (Luke 9:32). At Gethsemane, he found them asleep three times 'for their eyes were very heavy; and they did not know what to answer him' (Mark 14:40). Jesus did not get discouraged; why should we? The disciples were strong, rugged men, and who of us in the weariness of life has never known the body to take its revenge on the spirit. During a sea-crossing in bad weather Jesus was 'in the stern, asleep on the cushion' (Mark 4:38). These things put us in touch with the reality of the Gospel atmosphere, and help us to solve our own problems with more ease. In spite of it all, Jesus found a way to work on the disciples' hearts, for them to learn how to pray.

We must not say from this there is nothing for us to do, but just wait for the Spirit of Jesus to visit us. We must try to meet him, fight our way in at the narrow gate. If we are willing to make time for prayer, just to be alone with Our Lord, he will come to us. When he does come, we must make room for him, he will then begin to pray to the Father within us (John 14:6). In our difficulties in prayer, we have experience, our own and the Saints, the teaching of Our Lord in the Gospels and the tradition of the Church, to help us. Our main difficulty is just making time for prayer. We must never think that fatigue and activity remove all possibility of genuine prayer. Prayer is not meant to be something rare, reserved for people with leisure. It was hardly this that Our Lord meant when he said: 'Come to me, all you that labour and are burdened... and you shall find rest for your souls' (Matt. 11:28–29). We were created to love and be loved by God. If we lose contact with him in prayer, we cease to be human. St. Paul encourages us: 'Do not give up if trials come; and keep on praying' (Rom. 12:12).

2

I turned to the Lord God, seeking him by prayer.
(Dan. 9:3)

TO BE truly human we need a thirst for God. Our approach to God is bound to be personal, and there must be a personal life of prayer. Each of us has to find a way that suits our own temperament, but we can look to others for clues. Deep in each one of us lies the reality of God. Indeed, how could we go on seeking him, if we had not already found him? God promised his abiding presence to Moses and the Israelites (Deut. 31:6), and King David reminded his son Solomon: 'Is not the Lord your God with you?' (1 Chron. 22:18). St. Paul too told the Colossians: 'There is nothing but Christ in any of us' (Col. 3:11). Human history, which is the history of God in us, is still in progress. God's creative work still goes on, and Christ is present to us in everyone and everything. Our Lord told the Pharisees: 'The kingdom of God is here, within you' (Luke 17:21). Awareness of this omnipresence is the secret of all prayer; to be receptive and passive to that presence is the heart of prayer. There may be times when we seem to lose this presence, perhaps even to lose faith. On one such occasion St. Catherine of Siena complained to Our Lord: 'Where were you, Lord?' He replied: 'I was there with you all the time'.

Prayer, like love, is a gift. We have to make time for it, and learn to be passive and wait expectantly. It is the fruit of desire, not of our own techniques. It is not something we do; rather it comes from our being, something that springs from the depths, from the fountain of living waters welling from within. 'Do you not understand', wrote St. Paul, 'that you are God's temple, and that God's spirit has his dwelling in you' (1 Cor. 3:16). God is always near. Baron von Hugel used to say that he would be of no use, if he weren't. All we have to do, as the Liturgy tells us, is: 'Let us listen for the voice of the Lord, and enter into his peace'. Prayer of this kind can never isolate. It is in our union with Christ in prayer that we are drawn into the corporate life of the Church and our fellow men. How well Thomas Merton found this out, dying as he did outside his monastery at the other end of the world. He used to say that the Church could not fulfil her mission to transform and save without contemplation and interior prayer. To be contemplative is to be truly human, to live and love in a human way. 'As our priest Christ prays for us; as our head he prays in us; as our God, we pray to him, but let us recognize our voices in him, and his voice in us' (Liturgy for the Third Sunday of the year).

3

The hidden wisdom of God which we teach.
(1 Cor. 2:7)

FROM the time of their silently coming into this world, our ancestors loved to seek something of the meaning of life from the universal wonders of creation that surrounded them. Objects and acts acquired a value for them, and in so doing became real, because they participated after one fashion or another, in a reality that transcended them. With the present headlong advance in science and technology we have lost, at least in our waking moments, a reverence for material things, and as such have lost something of the meaning of living and loving that our ancestors learnt from the great universal symbols. There is a danger for us of equating spiritual maturity with intellectual development. This is not to despise reason. The problem arises in our ignoring the irrational for the rational, the unconscious for the conscious. For the best results we need both. Science is a child of the reason; culture encompasses, masters and gives form to all the depths of the unconscious and what lies hid in the past. Scientists in their research have to discover something that was previously unknown. Poets and artists, whilst remaining in the world of known things, enrich their quality and depth.

The Liturgy, in which we worship together, is a precious gift that stirs the inner depths of our being. How wise the Church is today in restoring her Liturgy to help stem the general decline in religion. It is in her Liturgy that she teaches us the timeless truths of reality. It is in her Rites, especially in the Mass, that we return to our roots, not only in the universe, but also in God. It is in her Liturgy that the Church unites all the deepest longings of the human race, the yearning for rebirth and infinite life. It is in her Liturgy that she teaches us to be human, not only by instructing our minds, but also by trying to make us see our place in the universe, by bringing us into contact with real fundamental things, matter, fire, water, oil, bread and wine – to love everything that is true and beautiful in a creation vibrating in motion and love. The Church tries to lead us to understand God, not only with our minds, but also with the whole of our being.

To lose contact with the symbol is to lose contact with the teaching of God himself, to lose the instinctive life of vision, and to a great extent to lose the Spirit of God. Symbols are never invented, they just happen. In its Greek origin a symbol denotes a throwing together of two such things that have something in common. It was used as a tally – two halves of a coin or piece of bone broken in two, when put together would give proof of identity of two persons. In its strict sense a symbol does not represent, but presents a truth. An external object is presented and makes contact with the within of our being. It responds to a need and fulfils a function of bringing to light the most hidden modalities of being. In so doing it makes clear ideas and emotions that could not otherwise be adequately expressed. It is a key to the hidden depths of our psyche, as well as to a deeper understanding of Scripture, music and art and to loving.

4

Jesus came up and touched them. Stand up, he said, do not be afraid.
(Matt. 17:7)

POPE PAUL VI went to meet his Redeemer on August 6th 1978, not on the mount of the Transfiguration, but high up in the Alban hills. Monsignor Bonicelli, Bishop of Albano, who was present at the death of Pope Paul, said his last words were that the death of a Pope is like that of any other man; it has something to say. Pope Paul's death certainly had something to say.

The secret of all living and dying is in loving, and Pope Paul was a very lovable man. He would be the last person to want me to give an account of his achievements and all he suffered. They can be read in various books and articles – his work of implementation of the Documents of the Second Vatican Council, his striving for world peace and Christian Unity, his tenacious care in preserving the Deposit of Faith and the Magisterium handed on to him as Christ's Vicar. He himself would say that is what you would expect from the Servant of the Servants of God. Truly he was the Servant of God, but above all he was a man of prayer.

The religious leaders of this country who met Pope Paul – Cardinal Basil Hume, the late Archbishop Michael Ramsey and Dr. Donald Coggan – all have spoken of the holiness of the man. Paul VI did not have the childlike simplicity of John XXIII, nor did he have the humility of St. Pius X, nor the deep insight of Pius XII. When you have lived with people you know what to look for in a man of God – his spirit of personal prayer. True, it is the Spirit of Christ who prays within us, as St. Paul says (Rom. 8:26–27), but he also told the Corinthians that it is precisely this spirit of prayer that forms us into the likeness and image of God (2 Cor. 3:18).

Just after his elevation to the See of Westminster in 1976, Abbot Hume in a sermon told his listeners to keep their eyes on the Holy Father. During his Pontificate I used to read with care the talks Pope Paul gave at his Wednesday public audiences. I developed a great love for the man, who became for me the most spiritual Pope of the century. I noticed how often he drew attention to the great need for 'personal prayer in this present age of the Church'. We all need to participate in the public act of worship in the Church as the people of God, in the Liturgy of the Mass and the Sacraments, and as Priests in the 'work of God' in the Divine Office. No other Pope has done so much for the reform of the Liturgy, and yet Pope Paul says: 'The Liturgy which is the official form of our religion, which is essentially social and ecclesial, presupposes and requires the spiritual contact with God in conscious and personal prayer'. I could go on quoting passage after passage in which he speaks of 'the importance of personal prayer', 'the interior moment of prayer', 'the joy of prayer'.

I came to see that the message of personal prayer was his favourite subject, and it turns up like a recurring theme of a great symphony. Pope Paul called it 'a great subject, like a cathedral'. There is one quotation I would like to impress on the mind; it was given on Wednesday June 2nd. 1976 in a public audience. 'Let us endeavour not to let ourselves be caught up in the religious and spiritual apathy which is so widespread today in our mundane and secularised world, and which seems to be an inevitable result of modern activism and of the overwhelming babel of public voices, but let us seek and adapt the programme of Christ's own formula: watch and pray'. His great gift was to watch and pray. He did not say in as many words, but implied that the danger of our age is to fall unknowingly into the heresy of Semi-Pelagianism condemned at the Council of Orange in 529. Pelagius unfortunately came from our land, and St. Jerome in a letter pictured him as 'being fed on Scotch oats'. He thought we could get along nicely on our own, without reference to God and contact with him through grace and prayer. The opposite is so true – for successful action we need to watch and pray.

The subject of prayer, like Christ himself, is so vast. Personal prayer is an experience of God 'infolding' us, folding us within. God created in us the need for himself. Prayer is this desire to cleave to him through his Son. It is the realization that Christ, the Son of God, entered this world, that he rose from the dead, that he is still a living and loving centre of radiation for all the energies of the world to meet, where we and the whole world are brought together. Prayer is seeing, it is a vision by which we see that all our being and becoming, all that we endure with faith and in love, our whole life and death itself, brings us closer to God; for he is at the heart of everything. Prayer is just the awareness of this living presence.

Although it is impossible for us to be thinking of God all the time, we do need set times, when we become receptive and passive to the influence of God, and for this we need to be quiet and alone, as it were open to God. Then we communicate with him, not only by word, but also by silence, when we become free to feel the Spirit of God, who is a Spirit of Love (Gal. 5:22). Religion must always find its ultimate in silence and love; without it there is only bustle and activity, no deep thought, no inner peace. This is not to

deny the need for action, we all have to do God's work, and
it is hard work. But where we have this gentle passivity and
inner need for God, he will be found outside in all we do.
The soul who finds God within, is bound to see him
reflected outside. I thank God for Pope Paul VI for
reflecting this. He died, as he wished, in the brilliant light
of Christ on the feast of the Transfiguration, August 6th.
And Jesus came and touched him and said: 'Stand up. Do
not be afraid'. Looking up he saw no one but only Jesus.

5

Come away to some lonely place all by yourselves and rest for a while.
(Mark 6:31)

GAUDETE Sunday is a day of rejoicing for me, since I was ordained to the Priesthood on that day in 1948. The Liturgy of the day is full of expectancy. Expectation is truly a Christian function. We should never forget our need for the absolute. It is because we can look to the beyond that we are able to find Christ in the present. This is God's gift, and St. Paul told the Galatians: 'I cannot bring myself to give up God's gift' (Gal. 2, 21). It is this that gives us 'the liberty we enjoy in Christ Jesus' (Gal. 2:4).

None of us can alter our temperaments and sometimes things get a little overpowering, and a withdrawal from our daily routine helps to balance things out. One of the best ways of doing this is to make a spiritual retreat. Today opportunities are given for making directed and guided retreats. It is also possible to have a preached retreat. Retreats do help us to find the right gradient for grace to flow to us. I was asked to preach such a retreat to my fellow Priests of the Northampton Diocese. The thoughts and words that follow were shared with them in the years 1974 and 1975. Before putting them to paper, I would like, by way of a preface, to relate a story as it was told to me. In a nutshell it presents the mystery of the cure for our ills and disorders. It was told to me by the late Dr. Franz Elkisch, and he added in his own inimitable way: 'It is a lovely story, James; so it seems to me'.

Once upon a time there was a drought in a district of China and the people made sacrifices and prayed to the nature gods, but they were not able to placate them and put them in a favourable mood. Then one person remembered that there was a wise old man some distance away; so the whole village went in a large procession to him and told him their troubles. 'Oh yes, yes, yes', he said, 'put some food outside my hut and you will have your rain in three days'. And so it happened. When they asked him how he did it, he replied: 'It's quite simple. You see it didn't rain when it should have rained, nature was out of order; so I put myself in order, and nature followed me. That's all'.

1

Look, I am standing at the door, knocking. If one of you hears me calling and opens the door, I will come in to share his meal, side by side with him.
(Rev. 3:20)

I suppose most of us are tossed about by a force greater than ourselves. This in itself is not a bad thing, since it is possible then to experience the almost physical presence of Christ clasping and leading us on. I am sure that if we are honest with ourselves, we have to confess that we are very much children of our own age; it is inevitable we should be. The Vatican Council, that opened on October 11th 1962, has affected all our lives. We are conscious of a deeper involvement in the Church in the modern world, and the interest we ought to show in renewal and all that concerns the Church today. But basic to all this concern, as the Council pointed out, is the love we should have for the word of God. 'For in the sacred books, the Father in heaven meets his children with great love and speaks with them; and the force and power in the word of God is so great that it remains the support and energy of the Church, the strength of faith for her sons and daughters, the food of the soul, the pure and perennial source of spiritual life' (Dogmatic Constitution on Divine Revelation). In this it points to the words of Our Lord: 'My mother and my brothers are those who hear the word of God and put it into practice' (Luke 8:21), and to those of St. Paul to Timothy: 'All scripture is inspired by God and can be profitably used... for guiding people's lives and teaching them to be holy' (2 Tim.3:16).

Bearing this in mind, and also St. Jerome's remark that to be ignorant of the Scriptures is to be ignorant of Christ, I have tried to base most of what I have to say on the foundation of the word of God. I am by no means a scriptural scholar, but I do have a great love for God's word; in fact I owe my own conversion to it. I found there not only God, but also myself. As a student I used Scripture for turning up texts to prove theses; and even though I had long passages read to me at the Divine Office and during meals, and had read the Bible from cover to cover, it was only in later life, in deeper moments of prayer, I realized it is the main branch, the only branch, that attaches us to Christ. Did he not say: 'Cut off from me you can do nothing'? And he goes on to say it is 'by means of the word I have spoken to you' that we not only bear 'fruit in plenty', but remain in him. 'Make your home in me, as I make mine in you' (John 15:1–6).

'Look, I am standing at the door, knocking, if one of you hears me calling and opens the door, I will come in' (Rev. 3:20). This scene from the Book of Revelation has been made popular by the pre-Raphaelite painter Holman Hunt. The Book of Revelation, like the whole of revelation, is an epic of Christian hope and faith in the Lord Jesus, who suffered and died, but is risen and now lives in glory. The words of Revelation close with the message: 'The one who guarantees these revelations repeats his promise: I shall indeed be with you soon. Amen; come, Lord Jesus' (Rev. 22:20). Our longing for the Risen Christ is so necessary; it is the basis for any spiritual life, and indeed for all I have to say.

'Look, I am standing at the door, knocking' (Rev. 3:20). We have the key to that door – the living word of God in Sacred Scripture. It was from my contact with Scripture that I gradually became aware of the reality of the living presence of Christ; an awareness that is so necessary for all true prayer. It was in middle life that I really began to see this, at the time when we begin to find within ourselves all that in youth we sought to find and conquer in the world outside. This awareness led me to a deeper insight into the word of God, deeper than the strict literal sense. It was then that I first came into contact with what has been called the Eternal Feminine, given to man as 'a helper fit for him' (Gen. 2:20). It is true God is neither male nor female; but then, as St. Thomas Aquinas explains, all that God creates has its perfection within himself.

The whole of Scripture is a womb, the fertile womb from which came not only Christ, but also the Church that gives life to us all. In our Latin days we used to sing on Holy Saturday that we were born 'ab immaculato divini fontis utero'. Right from the beginning 'ab initio et ante creata sum', it is the feminine, Sophia, the Wisdom of God, that gives life. Scripture, even apart from the love poems of the Song of Songs, depicts God's relationship with us as a sort of love relationship between husband and wife. Isaiah puts it this way: 'Like a young man marrying a virgin, so will the one who built you wed you, and as the bridegroom rejoices in his bride, so will your God rejoice in you' (Isaiah 62:5). Again he has that lovely passage: 'For your Maker is your husband, the Lord of hosts is his name; and the Holy One of Israel is your Redeemer, the God of the whole earth he is called. For the Lord has called you like a wife forsaken and grieved in spirit, like a wife of youth when she is cast off, says your God. For a brief moment I forsook you, but with great compassion I will gather you... with everlasting love I will have compassion on you, says the Lord, your Redeemer' (Isaiah 54:5–8). Speaking through Hosea, God says: 'Therefore I will hedge up her way with thorns; and I will build a wall against her, so that she cannot find her paths... Then she shall say, "I will go and return to my first husband, for it was better with me then than now' " (Hosea 2:6–7).

These experiences, expressed so beautifully in symbolism, were given directly to 'apostles and prophets'; but they were meant to be shared collectively throughout the ages by the whole Church, whose very foundation rests on the apostles and prophets (Eph. 2:20). We too in our own way share this divine relationship when we hearken to the word of God, and listen to him in our prayer and sacramental life. For in experiencing the profound symbolic contents of our being, we encounter the workings of God within us, who created us in his own image (Gen. 1:27).

2

It was you who created my inmost self,
And put me together in my mother's womb;
For all these mysteries I thank you:
For the wonder of myself, for the wonder of your works.

(Psalm 139:13–14)

In the theology of creation, I remember coming across that wonderful expression: Deus creat uniendo – God creates by uniting. All being is from God, and he is present to us in the very act of our being. To dwell on this gives joy to the reality of living and loving, and becomes an experience of the presence of God. The evil in and around us is due to the fact that we ignore this gift of ourselves, and then life and the world become hateful.

Life for all of us must be a mystery, something to be wondered at. It is also a voyage of discovery, and only the making of the voyage can help us live to the full and have a little insight to its meaning. True, life is a movement we are led into over a long period; in fact all the past is a preparation for it. What I am today must inevitably be the outcome of what has gone. But for this there has to be a receptivity, a passivity in each one of us capable of being activated, energized and developed. To a large extent that passivity comes from the positive side of a man's femininity, his Anima in Jungian terminology; I will come back to this shortly.

The half way stage in life is often so crucial. We find there so much nervous disturbance and mental depression, a sort of anorexia for living. In the first half of life we naturally go out to find our environment in an objective reality. Like the hero myth we set out to conquer the world, move out into society to fulfil a position in life, or find a suitable partner in marriage. In middle life these external ambitions no longer seem to satisfy. It is then we need to deepen our self knowledge, by turning to an inner reality that has remained unconscious for so long. Our Lord told Nicodemus that he needed to be born again. 'Nicodemus said, "How can a grown man be born? Can he go back into his mother's womb and be born again?". Jesus replied: "I tell you most solemnly , unless a man is born through water and the Spirit, he cannot enter the kingdom of God... Do not be surprised when I say: You must be born from above" ' (John 3:4–7). It is through this renewal that we begin to experience the mystery of life and find that God really exists, and begin to see that he reveals himself in Christ Jesus and that his Spirit lives in our hearts.

Fortunately for me at this time of life I came upon two of the greatest personalities who really affected the whole course and direction of my life. I owe a debt of gratitude to them both. Though of a different outlook on life, both helped to give me a deeper insight into my own being, which led me to an appreciation for the Sapientia of God and an abiding love for St. Paul and St. John. The men Fr. Pierre Teilhard de Chardin and Dr. Carl Gustav Jung were contemporaries, though perhaps neither knew the other. I am not an authority on either. Rather by insight both have helped to establish within me a spirituality that has given me a zest for living and loving, for taking part in the struggle that God wages in history, and for feeling the heart of his Son throbbing in the world.

In 1957, four years before he died, Jung told the world that all the outer aspects of his life had been accidental, only what was interior had proved to have had substance and a determining value. A person's normality is not the norm of society, but rather the norm of his own inner being. St. Paul was so convinced of this that he told the Corinthians: 'I have no mind that anybody should think of me except as he sees me, as he hears me talking to him' (2 Cor. 12:5). Yet at the same time he insisted that we have to work constantly at a spiritual renewal. 'Your mind must be renewed by a spiritual revolution so that you can put on the new self that has been created in God's way, in the goodness and holiness of the truth' (Eph. 4:23–24). And he adds: 'You have put on a new self which will progress towards true knowledge the more it is renewed in the image of its creator' (Col. 3:10).

My own great experiences have not been religious but rather psycho-religious, if I can coin the word. It was not until I had accepted myself and the contents of my inner life, that I was able to appreciate to the full what in the past I had taken so much for granted. In a book entitled 'Psychology and Alchemy' Jung lamented the fact that so few people ever experience the divine image as the innermost possession of their souls. Christ seems to meet them only from without, never within the soul; and that is why he said paganism was now so rampant.

We should always pray with optimism for the passion of living to the full. It is a fountain that springs up from within. Our Lord promised: 'The water that I shall give will turn into a spring inside him, welling up to eternal life' (John 4:14). May he preserve within us this impulse towards progress of fuller being, and may he at the same time direct this deep rooted urge towards himself. What paralyses life so much is failure to believe and failure to dare.

I am very attached to that old collect: Lord God, you have prepared for those who love you what no eye has seen, no ear has heard. Fill our hearts with your love, so that loving you above all and in all (ut te in omnibus et super omnia diligentes), we may attain your promises which the heart of man has not conceived (20th Sunday of the Year). 'For all these mysteries I thank you: for the wonder of myself, for the wonder of your works' (Psalm 139:14).

3

May the God of peace make you perfect and holy; and may you all be kept safe and blameless, spirit, soul and body, for the coming of our Lord Jesus Christ. God has called you and he will not fail you.

(1 Thess. 5:23)

Every one who comes into this world is in a sense a mystery. Every one is not only himself, he is unique, a being where the particular phenomena of life meet once and for all and never again in this life. In each of us the spirit is made flesh. In each of us the whole of creation suffers. In each of us a saviour is crucified and rises again. Yet the paradox is, no one is ever utterly himself. We carry within us the vestiges not only of our birth, but all that lies hid in the primeval world.

My grandfather on my father's side was Irish, a McDermott from Boyle, Co. Roscommon, my grandmother was a Scot, a McCreath from Glasgow. On my mother's side, her father was a school master from Yorkshire, named Taylor, her mother came from the farming stock of the Johnsons of Congleton; they settled and kept the School House at Diseworth in Derbyshire. My father was born in Wrexham, North Wales, where he met and married my mother. They made a home in Wolverhampton, where I was born.

It is from our mothers that we receive all that is best in life. My mother, though small in stature, was full of energy, with a strong faith in the divine. She came from a staunch Anglican family, but was received into the Catholic Church in the early years of married life. Always she found time for prayer, her Rosary, and Bible reading every night. Outgoing, she was ready to help and console others. It was from Mother Church too that I learnt so much during my early years. Paul Claudel, who had such a great love for the Church, said: 'The great book whose pages were open to me from which I could learn so much was the Church. Blessed be that great mother at whose knees I learnt so much'. This is a truth we all appreciate; the Church is the Sacrament of Christ, the mother who brings life to the daughters and sons of God. All through the ages she continues the mission of Christ and is animated by his Spirit.

It was my mother and the Church who nurtured my vocation. I left home in September 1935, at the age of thirteen, to become a Church student at Cotton College, North Staffs. There in historical studies and private reading I first learnt of the Cistercian monks and their glorious past as reflected in the Abbeys of Fountains, Rievaulx and Tintern and present day Mount Saint Bernard's. I entered the community of Mount Saint Bernard Abbey on the feast of St. Bernard, August 20th 1940, which took me, as I see it now, not from the world, but from myself. This led me into the womb of my own inner being, and gave me a passivity which was to grow into new life.

After my ordination to the Priesthood in 1948 I was asked by the Abbot, Dom Malachy Brasil, to help in the training of the Novices, whose numbers had increased after the war, teaching them Spirituality, The Holy Rule of St. Benedict, the Regulations and Constitutions, as well as initiating them in all the tasks of farm and house work. After eight years, those whom I had trained were free to take over, and I was able to give myself to the ordinary duties of monastic living, and was put in charge of landscaping the grounds and erecting the Calvary and the Lourdes Grotto. This gave me more time for thought and insight.

It was at this time that it fell to my lot on three consecutive years to give sermons on the various feasts of Our Lady. Monastic sermons, as those of St. Bernard, St Ailred, Guerric of Igny etc., were never preached, but always written and read. Working at these sermons, I became interested in the Eternal Feminine. I began to realize for the first time that the secret to life lies in a symbiosis, an enantiodromia – the running together of complementary opposites, the human and the divine, masculine and feminine, action and passion, east and west, light and darkness, conscious and unconscious, death and resurrection. By chance I came across Fr. Pierre Teilhard de Chardin and Dr. Carl Jung, and saw that they too were concerned with the same problem that faced me. For both of them the secret to life in its wholeness lay in a symbiosis, the complementary force of opposites to be sought and embraced within, and then lived in the world at large.

'May you all be kept safe and blameless, spirit, soul and body, for the coming of our Lord Jesus Christ' (1 Thess. 5:23). God does consolidate the work of his creation, particularly through the fusion of complementary opposites. On the eve of his death, Christ prayed for the unity of the divine with the human. 'I have given them the glory you gave to me, that they may be one as we are one. With me in them and you in me, may they be so completely one' (John 17:22–23). I found that this unity could be wonderfully enhanced by what Dr. Jung called his 'Individuation Process' and what Fr. Teilhard spoke of as a 'Process of Unanimisation'. These terms seemed to carry the same import for me. Both view everything from a single whole. Dr. Jung looks to our 'Wholeness' and Fr. Teilhard to our 'Complexification'. Both speak of two complementary forces fusing together to form the circle of wholeness. Dr. Jung expresses it in terms of an 'Inner and Outer', the unconscious and the conscious, uniting to form the 'Self ', the integrated being. Fr. Teilhard speaks of 'a Within and a Without', the growth of 'Passivities' and 'Activities', converging to form a 'Milieu Divin', Christ the true Self in men and women. The Self is the centre of our being, that also encloses the whole – spirit, psyche and soma.

The problems of an individual are connected with the great problems of society. An individual's attempt to solve his own problem is nothing less than an attempt to solve a universal problem. Neurosis is always self division, and today we are divided. On one hand our conscious and scientific mind wants to hang on to what can be grasped and calculated, while on the other our unconscious strives after cultural ideals that cannot be formulated in words or figures. Those who sat under the baton of Leopold Stokowski say he inspired them to play not only with their instruments, but also with their hearts. For the best results in life we need both science and culture. Science is the child of reason, culture encompasses, masters and gives form to all the depths of the beauty of the unconscious; together they help to create a well rounded personality. The unconscious only asserts itself when it is ignored. That is why our headlong advance in technology and science tends to foster a barbarism that is destructive not only physically and sexually, but also spiritually.

We are so prone to transfer onto others all the injustice and violence we inflict on our selves. St. John tells us a nobleman asked Our Lord to come down and heal his son 'ut descenderet et sanaret' (John 4:47). We do need to descend. The element of mystery demands a more symbolic, intuitive and affective approach than that provided by reason alone. Culture deals with signs and wonders, through them we learn to believe. We are told the father of the sick child asked when the boy began to recover. 'Yesterday at the seventh hour the fever left him', they said. The father realized that this was exactly the time when Jesus said: 'Your son will live' (John 4:52–53), and he and all his household believed. To have faith is to grow in stature. For in the nature of things everything that is of faith ascends, and all that ascends must eventually converge on Christ. 'May the God of peace make you perfect and holy; and may you all be kept safe and blameless, spirit, soul and body, for the coming of our Lord Jesus Christ. God has called you and he will not fail you' (1 Thess. 5:23).

4

Where the spirit of the Lord is, there is freedom. And we, with our unveiled faces reflecting like mirrors the brightness of the Lord, all grow brighter and brighter as we are turned into the image that we reflect; this is the work of the Lord who is Spirit.

(2 Cor. 3:18)

In his Priestly Prayer, which he made as a preparation for his Paschal Mystery, Our Lord prayed that he might always be in those who loved him (John 17:26). To love him, to desire to be one with him in the oneness of our being, spirit, soul and body, in the oneness of the Self, is to reflect his image. This is a living reality, as St. Paul reminded the Colossians: 'It was God's good pleasure to let all completeness dwell in him, and through him to win back all things,

whether on earth or in heaven, into union with himself'
(Col 1:19–20). Our desire to be one with Christ is not just a
pious wish to be projected into the future. He is with us
here and now. Indeed, to have sought him, is to have
already found him.

This I know is vision. But then how necessary vision is! It
gives an optimism for living and loving. You do need a
sense of vision for vision; that is why it is easier to radiate
than express in words. Even St. Paul experienced this, as
St. Peter pointed out: 'He always writes like this when he
deals with this sort of subject, and this makes some points
in his letter hard to understand' (2 Pet. 3:16).

Both Fr. Teilhard and Dr. Jung were fascinated by the
vision of wholeness and completion. Both found its fullest
expression was missing in our western world of today. Both
were drawn to the east, where they spent a considerable
time in research. Our western world thrives on a conscious,
active, personal level, and has lost contact with the
unconscious, passive, transpersonal level of the east. For
four years I had the privilege of living with and training two
Igbo Priests from Eastern Nigeria, and experienced their
wonderful gift of acceptance and passivity, the ability to be
lost in wonder and contemplation. One of these Priests, Fr.
Cyprian Michael Tansi, died in Leicester Royal Infirmary
on January 20th 1964. I was the last person to see him alive.
The canonical process for his beatification, to venerate his
memory, has been initiated in Rome. His compatriot, Fr.
Mark Ulogu, now lives in the Monastery of Our Lady of
Bemenda in the Cameroon.

For Fr. Teilhard the 'divina patiens' is the most fruitful
source of creative energy. The dark waters of Genesis were
formless till the Spirit of God touched them. The slime of
the earth was sterile till the Creator's hand formed it into a
living being. We too, passive in the grace forming hands of
God, grow into a milieu of the living God. 'And we, with
our unveiled faces reflecting like mirrors the brightness of

the Lord, all grow brighter and brighter as we are turned into the image that we reflect; this is the work of the Lord who is Spirit (2 Cor. 3:18). To neglect the deeper side of our being, to refuse to allow ourselves to be passive in the hands of God, is to lose the vision of wholeness.

God willed that wholeness should be brought to us through a Death and Resurrection, that of his divine Son. 'As he is the Beginning, he was first to be born from the dead, so that he should be first in every way; because God wanted all perfection to be found in him and all things to be reconciled through him and for him, everything in heaven and everything on earth, when he made peace by his death on the cross' (Col. 1:18–20). The Paschal Mystery of Our Lord's Death and Resurrection is not only the pattern of our spiritual lives, but also of our psycho-somatic as well. Our psychic system is self regulatory, it experiences a continual emergence to new life through a death and resurrection. In the history of the human race conscious-ness, under the creative activity of God, emerges into new life. In every individual consciousness re-experiences its emergence from the unconscious in the growth of child-hood. Every night in sleep we die with the sun, sinking back to the depths of the unconscious, rising again with it in the morning to begin the new day. The whole of life is based on the complementary function of regression and progression, a death and resurrection. St. Paul told the Philippians that Christ 'will transfigure these wretched bodies of ours into copies of his glorious body. He will do that by the same power with which he can subdue the whole universe' (Phil. 3:21), that is, through his Death and Resurrection. Christ by virtue of his Incarnation, crowned by his Death and Resurrection, became the living centre of his creation.

In St. Paul's vision it is Christ who 'holds all things in unity' (Col. 1:17). Yet in his vision of oneness he saw that woman had a necessary part to play in bringing it to completion, for 'when the appointed time came, God sent his Son, born of a woman' (Gal. 4:4). Jung too, when he came to formulate his own vision of Individuation, saw how necessary woman is in helping to lead man to salvation. Man's conscious life by nature is masculine, so to compensate for this the main contents of his unconscious are feminine, and of course vice versa for woman. In his search for wholeness and Individuation a man needs the cooperation of his own archetypal woman, someone who is part of his very self. Jung called her the Anima, the soul of man who gives life to his personality; the complementary partner of woman he called the Animus. The Anima and Animus lead us to maturity 'until we become the perfect Man, fully mature with the fulness of Christ himself ' (Eph. 4:13). These were some of the last words written by St. Paul, but they re-echo what he wrote years before to the Corinthians: 'Where the Spirit of the Lord is, there is freedom. And we, with our unveiled faces reflecting like mirrors the brightness of the Lord, all grow brighter and brighter as we are turned into the image that we reflect; this is the work of the Lord who is Spirit' (2 Cor. 3:18).

5

When Jesus reached the official's house and saw the flute-players, with the crowd making a commotion, he said, 'Get out of here; the little girl is not dead, she is asleep'. And they laughed at him. But when the people had been turned out he went inside and took the little girl by the hand; and she stood up.

(Matt. 9:23–25)

I find it interesting that Dr. Jung should define the Anima as the personification of man's unconscious in general, and of course the Animus for woman's. So few are aware of their unconscious, and so of their Anima and Animus. And yet they do have a saving role to play in leading us to

84

wholeness in our relationship with God. St. Matthew tells us Our Lord 'went inside' and 'took the little girl by the hand' and raised her up; she was not dead, only sleeping (Matt. 9:25). The Anima has so much to give and yet when asleep can cause so much havoc in a man's life. By nature she is his contra-sexual partner and through her he experiences the beauty of love.

Love is the most universal, most formidable and mysterious of all cosmic energies, a force in everyone's life. Morris West describes the problem in his novel 'The Devil's Advocate'. The story centres round an English Monsignor, who on being told by a consultant that he has an incurable cancer and only a short time to live, suddenly realizes that his life, the greater part of which he has spent in the Curia Offices at the Vatican, has been empty, because he never learnt to love. On his return to Rome he is sent as a Devil's Advocate to look into the past of a man whom his followers look upon and venerate as a Martyr – Saint. He discovers this man was a deserter from the Allied Forces, had fathered a child, and was leader of the Patriots in their anti-Nazi activities. In so doing he comes into contact with an ordinary type of Bishop, a lax Priest, a loose-living Contessa, a cynical and drunken doctor and a homosexual artist. These personalities react as symbols on his unconscious, and he not only learns how to love through them, but dies trying to save a man's life; which event finally brings all these characters to a higher degree of consciousness and love.

We are told Our Lord 'went inside' and took the girl by the hand. The Anima is a man's luminous guide, through her he is led to embrace his unconscious and comes to accept himself as he really is. She is an archetype, an imprint that God has planted within him, a collective image, by which he apprehends the nature of the feminine and the mystery of love. Jung was at pains to point out that the Anima also brings to light the dark shadow qualities with all the traits of immaturity. The danger lies in repressing the Anima, and not having a proper regard for women. It is then she is likely to act as a seductress manifesting herself in moods, fantasies and emotional outbursts. But when she is accepted and embraced as a partner, her power to harm is lessened. In her positive role she stimulates all the artistic gifts of man and all his creative beauty, she gives warmth to his affections and excites him to love and prepares him for his experience with woman. She is the symbol of all that is feminine, and leads man to a love for Our lady, the Church and Sacred Scripture.

Those who experience and live this relationship know it does not alienate from the world of reality; but it can enrich and broaden a personality. In the well rounded man his Anima is his partner, leading him, not downwards, but in an ever upward and forward movement. Even an affair with a particular woman can never destroy such a man. He knows he can never completely possess her; for he already has in the depths of his own psyche what he seeks to possess.

The mystical path of love has always held an attraction; but it is only the feminine that can make it possible. She is the guide who leads the mystic to union with God, for we all stand before God as the spouse and bride. That is why Yahweh in the Canticle of Isaiah sings: 'For Yahweh takes delight in you and your land will have its wedding. Like a young man marrying a virgin, so will the one who built you wed you, and as a bridegroom rejoices in his bride, so will your God rejoice in you' (Isaiah 62:4–5). St. John tells us our love is always a response to divine love (1 John 4:19), and the great joy in the life of vision is always to be open to receive love, to let oneself be loved by God as well as our fellow human beings. Such love must always be fruitful, because 'whoever remains in me, with me in him, bears fruit in plenty' (John 15:5).

My little children, I am in travail over you afresh, until I can see Christ's image formed in you ! *(Gal. 4:19)*

St Paul loved to see the whole of creation as being held together by Christ and in Christ; he is the main corner stone (Eph. 2:20). Everything in heaven and on earth has been created for Christ (Eph. 1:9–10). And so it is in Christ, the Incarnate Word, God and Man, that we and the universe find our fulfilment. 'As he is the Beginning, he was first to be born from the dead, so that he should be first in every way; because God wanted all perfection to be found in him and all things to be reconciled through him and for him, everything in heaven and everything on earth' (Col. 1:18–20). The mystery of the Incarnation lies at the heart of God's creativity and his plan of Redemption. Yet these two great mysteries were made possible only through the openness and the beautiful expression of the feminine. 'When the appointed time came, God sent his Son, born of a woman, born a subject of the Law, to redeem the subjects of the Law and to enable us to be adopted as sons... God has sent the Spirit of his Son into our hearts: the Spirit that cries, "Abba, Father" '(Gal. 4:4–6). By her passive act of surrender Mary conceived and bore her Son and presented him to us. In so doing she became, not only the Mother of God, but also the Mother of the Church and our Mother too. Pope John Paul II has made this the general theme of his recent Encyclical Letter 'Redemptoris Mater'.

It is Mary's vocation to give us Christ and make him present to us. For God 'has chosen us out, in Christ' (Eph. 1:4), he 'has created us in Christ Jesus' (Eph. 2:10), 'we are limbs of his body; flesh and bone, we belong to him' (Eph. 5:30). Better than St. Paul, Our Lady can say: 'My little children, I am in travail over you afresh, until I can see Christ's image formed in you!' (Gal. 4:19). To be formed in Christ, we must be formed in some way in the feminine, in Mary too. For we advance to Our Lord by the same way he took to come to us, through the woman, Mary his Mother. In Mary the whole of creation became the sanctuary of God, and in Mary too we find not only Christ, but also the whole of creation. Like her we have to let our own passivities be energized and activated by the Spirit of Christ (Luke 1:35). It is the passive that releases all the energy for life. The darkness of our own passivities is full of presences. This darkness, like Mary's womb, is heavy with promise, which the soul can illuminate and animate with the divine presence.

'Mary', says Vatican II, 'has made an entry in depth into the history of salvation' (De Ecclesia). There is so much in life that has deep meaning, yet few are willing to pierce the interior depths of their being. Devotion to Our Lady is so necessary for our spiritual and psychical growth. All true Catholic piety must also be piety to Our Lady. Even Dr. Jung saw this and deprecated the barrenness of a belief that lacked the cult of the feminine. Indeed, both Our Lady and the Church, in their mission as woman and mother, are identical.

On the feast of Our Lord's Presentation, February 2nd 1974, Pope Paul VI published an Apostolic Exhortation, 'Marialis Cultus', to honour Mary. In it he writes: 'From the moment when we were called to the See of Peter, we have constantly striven to enhance devotion to the Blessed Virgin Mary, not only with the intention of interpreting the sentiments of the Church and our own personal inclination, but also, as is well known, this devotion forms a very noble part of the whole sphere of that sacred worship in which there intermingle the highest expressions of wisdom and of religion, and which is therefore the primary task of the people of God'. He then shows how devotion to Mary, based on Sacred Scripture, should find its full expression in the Liturgy and also, which I find encouraging, in the psycho sociological field in which we live and work.

Mary is like the dawning that ever rises out of the depths, stretching out to the future. She touches the depths of our being, the feminine that is so necessary in all our lives, both women and men. Priests and Religious need to be more conscious of their inner femininity, if they are to lead others to love God and the whole of creation in a more sublime way. We all need to love, if our lives are not to be empty, frustrated and unfulfilled.

On a deeper level than our own, Mary experienced the journey of the dark night common to all the redeemed. We have only to think of her prenuptial pregnancy, her flight into Egypt, the loss of her Son at the age of twelve, and his reminder that he must concern himself with the work of his Father. We recall the words of Our Lord when the woman in the crowd extolled him (Luke 11:27–28), and again the words: 'who is my mother?' (Matt. 12:48). Significant too is the title she gives herself, she is 'the handmaid of the Lord' (Luke 1:38). Her blessedness comes not from action, but from the passivity of what matured in her womb (Luke 1:42).

So often it is the simple things in life that stimulate. That is why Dr. Jung saw the symbol as a grace, a liberating grace. The most noble and thoughtful souls, in response to the request of Mary, are moved to piety by the Rosary. Indeed, the whole of life is Christianized in the development within us of the 'Hail Mary'. All that I have said is so beautifully presented in the symbolism of our Rosary. The beads lie jumbled up in our pockets, so symbolical of the chaos in our lives and our struggle for freedom. Take the beads out of the pocket by the Crucifix and lay them on the ground, and the pear shape of the uterus, with the maximum space at the top, becomes apparent. Take the Crucifix and place it in the centre of the womb, and the mandala, the magic circle, is complete; the divinity is incarnate within us. Christ, the Word of God, miraculously entered the womb of Mary, and our immersion there too, though mystical, is none the less real.

7

My children, our love is not to be just words or mere talk, but something real and active... Let us love one another since love comes from God and everyone who loves is begotten by God and knows God. Anyone who fails to love can never have known God, because God is love... No one has ever seen God; but as long as we love one another God will live in us and his love will be complete in us. **(1 John 3:18 and 4:7–12)**

St. John's vocation was to live his Beloved Master's call to love. For him love is the one real need of every human being, the only satisfactory answer to the problem of living. In his Second Letter he says we ought 'to live a life of love' (2 John 1:6). The word he uses in Greek has the idea of walking in love, wandering around, as it were finding it and embracing it. Sadly today so many in their search for it seem to have lost it. It is a passion so many crave for, and so few really attain. And yet love is the most universal of all cosmic energies. It penetrates the inner recesses of all creation, because it radiates the very nature of God who 'is love' (1 John 4:8). That is why whatever we find beautiful in loving has to be in some way in God, and why all loving has the characteristic of God himself.

Shakespeare was prompted to open his 'Twelfth Night; or What You Will' with the words: 'If music be the food of love, play on'. I used to think love was something amorphous; most people had a vague idea what it was, but no one could define it for me. True, it is a subject that is difficult to analyse without becoming too emotional and sentimental or too cold and pragmatic. The artist will always find it easier to paint and carve and sing about than words coming from the pen of a scholar. Strange too for me was the fact that so many of those engaged in mystical experiences of love and could describe them were for the most part celibates, St. Teresa of Avila, St. John of the Cross, St. Catherine of Siena, Dame Julian of Norwich and many of our English Mystics. They seemed to be able to experience and find love everywhere.

I know now to believe in love is to have an insight into the very nature of oneself and indeed of God himself. Love is by nature Trinitarian; it is a union, a oneness that springs from a living relationship. Love is not only the source of all things but is in all things. St. Thomas Aquinas lays down this principle at the very start of his thesis 'De Amore', on love, in his 'Summa Theologica'. He writes: 'Dicendum quod amor naturalis non solum in viribus animae vegetativae, sed in omnibus potentiis animae, et etiam in omnibus partibus corporis, et universaliter in omnibus rebus' (1.11 Quaest. 26). To be certain of its presence in ourselves, we have to assume its presence, at least in an inchoate form, in everything that is. Love is a synthesis that unites, something which St. Paul told the Corinthians emerges and grows and can never be destroyed (1 Cor. 13:13). It is a force that everyone, even Priests and Religious, have to struggle with, like Jacob wrestling with the angel. Jacob called the place Peniel saying: 'For I have seen God face to face, and yet my life is preserved' (Gen. 32:30). We have to find a place for love in our lives; if we fail, it is to our detriment. 'Anyone who fails to love can never have known God, because God is love' (1 John 4:8). These are the words of the one who lay with his head on the bosom of Christ (John 13:23).

The secret of life lies in the wonderful balance of complementary opposites. The tension that results from the union of opposites is an energy that is ever recreative. Dr. Jung never failed to assert that psychologically the opposite to love is not hate, but the will to power; so that where love is lacking the will to power will be paramount, a fault in the lives of many celibates, who never learn how to love.

So few really love because so few find the oneness of love in the depths of everything that is. For most people love can only be experienced in an embrace and all the physical attractions that may go with it. But inspite of all its beauty, this can be so passing, it comes and goes. There is an inner force of love that is ever recreative and is always present in the oneness of all that is. For this reason love does not enfold, it infolds from within. In his plan for fruitfulness, God seems to need the passivity and receptivity of our creaturely nature. Indeed, the whole of creation is created as openness to God (Hosea 2:16); it is this that makes love a feminine mystery. God does communicate himself to the human heart in the subjective experience of love. 'God is love and anyone who lives in love lives in God, and God lives in Him' (1 John 4:16). It is the feminine in all of us, women and men, that makes this a living experience. St. Paul says that this love is 'made visible in Christ Jesus our Lord' (Rom. 8:39).

A man's power to love is always stimulated by the feminine; this is as true for a Priest or Religious as for any other man. A Priest needs to be more aware of his inner reality, his numen, of his own Anima, if he is to be integrated, if he is to understand himself and help others with their problems. It is true he may become aware of her through a particular woman; but as long as she is seen and recognized as a projection and is withdrawn, she cannot utterly destroy him.

The more conscious we are of our own femininity the more we will be aroused by an adoring love. St. John says that such a love is not 'just words or mere talk, but something real and active' (1 John 3:18). It is constituted by the living presence of Christ, and the paradox is 'as long as we love one another God will live in us' (1 John 4:12). This is a treasure to embrace, for Christ is the binding force behind it. And since, as St. Paul says, 'he is your life' (Col. 3:4), united in Christ a further sense of oneness and togetherness is formed. Formed in Christ, such a love is timeless and spaceless, for it is infinite, and as such transcends man and woman; it is an eternal love (2 Cor. 4:18).

With our own femininity we can experience the plenitude of love. From this love a purity is engendered that blossoms in a chaste contact with the oneness of love, that is the same in all. For 'there is only Christ: he is everything and he is in everything' (Col. 3:11). True we cannot deny our feelings. But if we love in Christ and with Christ, Christ's Spirit will direct our love. The Mystical Christ in the Church and in the world is still in the state of becoming. And for this he depends on the feminine mystery of love in all our lives. Love is a vision. It is a flame that bursts into life.

8

Keep as your pattern the sound teaching you have heard from me, in the faith and love that are in Christ Jesus. You have been trusted to look after something precious; guard it with the help of the Holy Spirit who lives in us.

(2 Tim. 1:13–14)

The Church opens the wonderful season of Lent with the prayer: 'Through our Lenten observance, Lord, deepen our understanding of the mystery of Christ, and make it a reality in the conduct of our lives' (First Sunday of Lent). The element of the mysterious always draws. We are led to believe that the mysterious is a reality that cannot be grasped by the reason and the understanding. But if we analyse the word 'mystery', we see it comes from a Greek verb to close the eyes and shut the mouth. The truth is, the mysterious can only be perceived from the quietness of the within. So often in the quietness of our lives we fail to appreciate 'the unfathomable riches of Christ' (Eph. 3:9), and as a result there are times when the mystery of Christ and his infinite mercy in the divine Redemption become nebulous. But the Church is always at hand to give us support. She tells us in her recent Constitution 'On the Church in the Modern World' that she 'believes that the

93

key, the centre and purpose of the whole of mankind's history is to be found in its Lord and Master'.

St. Paul too has the same answer to our problem. For him everything is resolved 'in Christ Jesus'. The expression runs like a refrain all through his Letters, a hundred and sixty four times in all, and can be found in each of his Letters, except the one to Titus. Christ was for St. Paul a living experience (Gal. 2:20), and he longed to share this experience with others. He knew from his own life that the elements of the spiritual life are always found within; they are there all the time and have to be uncovered. His own experience of Christ was a gradual growth. How different was his early experience expressed in his Letter to the Galatians from that of his Letters written in captivity, at the end of his life !

In his first Letter, probably that to the Galatians, the most personal and the one in which we detect so clearly his character in which he proclaims: 'it is Christ that lives in me' (Gal. 2:20), he describes his conversion, his own vision and experience, affirming that he did not receive it or learn it from any man, but 'it came to me by a revelation from Jesus Christ' (Gal 1:12). This revelation he told the Galatians, abrogated the Mosaic Law, bestowing a law of liberty and love open to Jew and Gentile alike, making them justified, not by circumcision, but through faith. It is 'through faith in Jesus Christ' (Gal. 2:16) that we all become the children of God, and 'baptized in Christ's name' (Gal. 3:27) we all become 'one person in Jesus Christ' (Gal. 3:28). This experience of Christ 'yields a harvest of love, joy, peace, patience, kindness, generosity, forbearance, gentleness, faith, courtesy, temperateness, purity (Gal. 5:22–23).

This experience of Christ led St. Paul gradually to rethink the whole of his past life, his reading of the Scriptures and his view of the world and history. So in his Letter to the Romans he began to identify his experience of the Gospel with 'the mystery, hidden from us through countless ages, but now made plain' (Rom. 16:25–26) through Christ. His conclusion therefore is, that Christ is the climax of salvation history, indeed of all history. All creation reveals God; and all who live in Christ become the children of God. Moreover, the whole aspiration and travail of nature is pervaded and aided and graced by 'the Spirit of God' (Rom. 8:9). The whole of nature moves towards fulfilment in Christ, since 'we are all assured that everything helps to secure the good of those who love God, those whom he has called in fulfilment of his design' (Rom. 8:28).

In the light of what God had done in the Christ event, Christians were to accept through faith and realize in their lives 'the mystery' of Christ's Death and Resurrection. This became the essential theme of his Letters to the Corinthians. 'The chief message I handed on to you, as it was handed on to me, was that Christ, as the scriptures had foretold, died for our sins; that he was buried, and then, as the scriptures had foretold, rose again on the third day... That is our preaching, mine or theirs as you will; that is the faith which has come to you... Christ has risen from the dead, the first fruits of all those who have fallen asleep; a man had brought us death, and a man should bring us resurrection from the dead; just as all have died with Adam, so with Christ all will be brought to life' (1 Cor. 15:3–22). It is only in Christ that we find the strength to go beyond the self centred existence common to all nature. That is why he shows the Corinthians that their problems in community life, partisan zeal, their gross immorality, their difficulties in courtship and married life, food offered to idols and disorders in the Eucharist can only be settled in Christ. For life is nothing else than the paradox of Christ: 'Weakness brought him to the cross, but the power of God brought him to life' (2 Cor. 13:4). By dying with Christ the Christian rises to a new life 'everything has become new about him' (2 Cor. 5:17). The Christian life is not just a mere moral code. The moral part is simply the necessary result of living 'the mystery' in the newness of life. 'God was in Christ, reconciling the world to himself' (2 Cor. 5:19), so that love, the greatest of the virtues, should always prevail. 'We shall never have finished with charity' (1 Cor. 13:8).

It was towards the end of his life that the world and his experience of living 'the mystery' were to take on a deeper meaning for St. Paul. And so in his Letters to the Philippians, Colossians and Ephesians, written in captivity, he felt the need 'of publishing to the world the plan of this mystery' (Eph. 3:9). This mystery, the design of God, conceived from all eternity, is revealed in the Gospel to save the whole world and women and men without distinction of race, forming them in Christ, in the unity of his Mystical Body.

Philippi was St. Paul's first conquest on European soil and always his favourite Church. In this unlearned, simple Roman Colony he found docile minds and loving hearts, and so he opens his heart to them. 'You are close to my heart, and I know you all share my happiness in being a prisoner, and being able to defend and assert the truth of the gospel' (Phil. 1:7). 'There is nothing I do not write down as loss compared with the high privilege of knowing Christ Jesus, my Lord; for love of him I have lost everything' (Phil. 3:8). It is in this Letter that he gives us the finest of his Christological passages: 'Yours is to be the same mind which Christ Jesus shewed. His nature is, from the first, divine, and yet he did not see, in the rank of Godhead, a prize to be coveted; he dispossessed himself, and took the nature of a slave, fashioned in the likeness of men, and presenting himself in human form' (Phil. 2:5–7). To know Jesus Christ, to be in Christ Jesus, is to share his mind. Our knowledge of Christ helps us to live joyously, so that we can find the world permeated with the divine values of truth, goodness, righteousness and excellence. 'All that rings true, all that commands reverence, and all that makes for right; all that is pure, all that is lovely, all that is gracious in the telling; virtue and merit, wherever virtue and merit are found – let this be the argument of your thoughts' (Phil. 4:8).

In his Letter to the Colossians St. Paul began to develop the theme of 'the mystery' in the world, by restoring to Christ his part in the creation and the ordering of the world, enthroning him as the Pantokrator. Christ, the image of the Father, is the first born of all creatures, the author, preserver and the end of all things. 'Yes, in him all created things took their being, heavenly and earthly... They were all created through him and in him; he takes precedency of all, and in him all subsist' (Col. 1:16–17). Christ is thus the divine exemplar, the universal archetype, the exemplary, the efficient and final cause of all created things. St. Paul knew the Colossians prided themselves as philosophers, and so he shows them that his own philosophy is based not on human traditions alone. His 'mystery' is the secret he had received from God: 'Christ among you, your hope of glory' (Col. 1:27). This 'mystery' is inseparable from the salvation of the world, for the world and every creature in it has to be perfect in Christ Jesus. Indeed, all completion, 'the pleroma', dwells in Christ. 'In Christ the whole plenitude of Deity is embodied and dwells in him, and it is in him you find your completion' (Col. 2:9–10). 'It was God's good pleasure to let all completeness dwell in him, and through him to win back all things, whether on earth or in heaven, into union with himself' (Col. 1:19–20).

It was in his last Letter, to the Ephesians, that St. Paul was to bring his vision and experience of 'the mystery' to its final conclusion, by showing how the world and the Church in the world form 'the pleroma' the complement of Christ. And so he writes: 'It was his loving design, centred in Christ, to give history its fulfilment by resuming everything in him, all that is in heaven, all that is on earth, summed up in him' (Eph. 1:9–10). Christ is the Pantokrator and Consummator of all things in the universe. God 'raised Christ from the dead, and bade him sit on his right hand above the heavens, high above all princedoms and powers… and every name that is known, not in this world only, but in the world to come. He has put everything under his dominion, and made him the head to which the whole Church is joined, so that the Church is his body, the completion of him who everywhere and in all things is complete' (Eph. 1:20–23). This then is 'the mystery', the plan of salvation conceived by God from all eternity, by which the whole universe and all of us are saved by the mediation of Christ, and by our own mystical union with him. St. Paul claims with pride: 'you see how well I have mastered this secret of Christ's' (Eph. 3:4), and why he considers it such a wonderful privilege 'of publishing to the world the plan of this mystery' (Eph. 3:9), 'of making known to the Gentiles the unfathomable riches of Christ' (Eph. 3:8), the fruit of which measured 'in all its breadth and length, the height and depth' is 'the love of Christ, to know what passes knowledge. May you be filled with all the completion God has to give' (Eph. 3:18–19).

9

You have probably heard how I have been entrusted by God with the grace he meant for you, and that it was by a revelation that I was given the knowledge of the mystery, as I have just described it very shortly. If you read my words, you will have some idea of the depths that I see in the mystery of Christ   *(Eph. 3, 2–4)*

There are times, I am sure, when we are inclined to think that our own personal experiences make us somehow different from those around us. Personal experiences do not divide, for it is precisely in the depths that unity lies. Often too we may feel that to be concerned with oneself, be it with one's Individuation Process, the formation of wholeness or one's completeness in Christ, would seem to isolate and create a veil of self centredness. The truth is just the opposite.

The mystic, indeed anyone who really thinks, always has to face this problem of the one and the many, the self and the other, the I – thou relationship. St. Paul worked it out for himself. He is the model for us all. Writing to the Corinthians he said: 'What we have received is no spirit of worldly wisdom'; and therefore 'mere man with his natural gifts cannot take in the thoughts of God's Spirit; they seem mere folly to him, and he cannot grasp them, because they demand a scrutiny which is spiritual' (1 Cor. 2:12–14).

St. Paul had such a wonderful love for the person of Christ. Like us, he never knew Our Lord in the flesh. All his knowledge and love came from within himself, from revelation (Eph. 3:2–4). It was because of his vision and experience of Christ that he undertook numerous perilous missionary voyages, that he preached in Jewish synagogues, before learned philosophers at Athens, before Roman Procurators, why he suffered persecution, imprisonment and finally bore witness to his vision by martyrdom. He complained to the Galatians and Corinthians that he lacked all the splendour of eloquence, the charm of language and the authority of wisdom. 'So much wiser than men is God's foolishness; so much stronger than men is God's weakness... No, God has chosen what the world holds foolish, so as to abash the wise, God has chosen what the world holds weak, so as to abash the strong... no human creature was to have any ground for boasting, in the presence of God. It is from him that you take your origin, through Christ Jesus, whom God gave us to be all our wisdom, our justification, our sanctification, and our atonement' (1 Cor. 1:25–30). 'I had no thought of bringing you any other knowledge than that of Jesus Christ, and of him as crucified... God's power, not man's wisdom, was to be the foundation of your faith' (1 Cor. 2:2–5).

He lived with the vision of Christ and burnt with the desire to share his innermost conviction with all women and men, so that 'the mystery' of Christ might not only be known, but experienced by everyone. He told the Colossians: 'I would bring courage to their hearts; I would see them well ordered in love, enriched in every way with fuller understanding, so as to penetrate the secret revealed to us by God the Father, and by Jesus Christ... Go on, then, ordering your lives in Christ Jesus our Lord, according to the tradition you have received of him. You are to be rooted in him, built up on him, your faith established in the teaching you have received, overflowing with gratitude' (Col. 2:2–7). That is why the person who has Christ has everything, nothing is wanting. Christ then becomes 'all our wisdom, our justification, our sanctification, and our atonement' (1 Cor. 1:30).

St. Paul's one prayer for his converts was: 'May he, out of the rich treasury of his glory, strengthen you through his spirit with a power that reaches your innermost being. May Christ find a dwelling-place, through faith, in your hearts; may your lives be rooted in love, founded on love. May you and all the saints be enabled to measure, in all its breadth and length and height and depth, the love of Christ, to know what passes knowledge. May you be filled with all the completion God has to give' (Eph. 3:16–19).

For this reason St. Paul made the whole secret of our formation consist in the practical knowledge and living of 'the mystery' of Christ in love. This too was the prayer of Our Lord at the Last Supper: 'Eternal life is this: to know you, the only true God, and Jesus Christ whom you have sent' (John 17:3). Only three times was the voice of the Father heard in the Gospels, and each time it was to say: 'This is my Son, the Chosen One. Listen to him' (Luke 9:35). He was the person born of Mary, nurtured at Bethlehem and Nazareth, grew in age and wisdom, learnt from his mother's knee, at the feet of his teachers and priests. Like us, he needed the support of friendship and love, as we see in the Gospels. On this level, he was just like us. But he was something more by the power of his Incarnation, his Death and Resurrection. He is the centre, the force that can subject all things to himself, the origin and the term of all creation, what St. John calls 'the Alpha and the Omega' (Rev. 22:13). Not only do we have a relationship with him as a member of the human race, but he has a deeper relationship with the whole of creation, because there is something of Christ in everything. 'There is only Christ', St. Paul told the Colossians, 'he is everything and he is in everything' (Col. 3:11). By our contact with him, we are brought into contact with the whole world.

The beauty of it all is, the more we live in this awareness and in our love for Christ, the more he lives in us; and the more he lives in us, the more we become united with all our fellow human beings (John 17:22–23). St. Paul told the Corinthians this is something we all have to work at. 'Surely your own conscience will tell you that Christ is alive in you, unless, somehow, you fail at the test' (2 Cor. 13:5). He was so convinced that we 'are all one person in Jesus Christ'

(Gal. 3:28). The more we personalize ourselves in Christ, the more we unite ourselves to the whole Christ.

Christianity alone can preserve the aim of all true mysticism, to find unity, becoming one with the other, without losing one's own personality. St. Paul, whom we have followed so carefully, saw that there is a single pattern running through history, the growth of Christ. He summed it all up by saying: 'Christ is all, and in all' or as Monsignor Knox translates it: 'There is nothing but Christ in any of us' (Col. 3:11). God's creative work still goes on. Christ is enshrined in all the beauty and the wonder of the world and his love gives life. Through the oneness of ourselves, and in our oneness together, we gather up at the same time everything into a single soul, that of the living Christ.

10

Something appeared to them that seemed like tongues of fire; these separated and came to rest on the head of each of them. They were all filled with the Holy Spirit.

(Acts 2:3–4)

Fr. Teilhard de Chardin went to meet his Redeemer on Easter Sunday 1955. A month before he died, he said that what had given him so much joy in his prayer life was that when he meditated on the reality of God and the world, a blaze of such brilliance appeared before him, that everything was seen to be alight. This is to speak in symbolism, but symbols are the very substance of our spiritual lives, they widen our experience of God. The author of the Letter to the Hebrews speaks about God confirming his witness 'with signs and marvels and miracles of all kinds, and by freely giving the gifts of the Holy Spirit' (Heb. 2:4).

It is precisely because childhood is drawn to the symbol, that it has about it that freshness, spontaneity and graciousness. For the child, the night journey through forests, caverns and seas, meeting the dragon, fighting for the princess and living together happily ever after, are the unconscious strivings of its whole being. Our ancestors too in their adult years loved to seek something of the meaning of life from the great universal symbols that surrounded them. Objects and acts acquired a value for them, and in so doing became real, because they participated after one fashion or another in a reality that transcended them. Among the countless number of stones one became sacred, impregnated with a numinous or religious power, by virtue of its symbolic shape or origin; thunderstone, believed to have fallen from the sky, pearl because of its coming from the depths of the sea. Other stones were sacred because they were once the scene of a theophany, as the bethel that served Jacob for a bed, or because a sacrifice or covenant had consecrated them, and Laban said to Jacob: 'May this cairn be a witness between us today' (Gen. 31:48). We may not have the same appreciation for symbolism as they did; but the symbol can never be completely extirpated from our lives, because we carry deep within us the vestiges of all that has gone.

There is always the danger, when we lose contact with the image and symbol, of losing contact with the teaching of God himself, and also of losing the instinctive, intuitive life of vision, and the Spirit of God. To lose sight of the Holy Spirit is to lose the very meaning of Christianity. If the Holy Spirit is forgotten or neglected, Christianity becomes no more than a moralizing cult. The Holy Spirit is not only the soul of the Church, but also the animating force behind our every Christian act and endeavour. Without him the Mystical Body would be a mere society, and all its vitality reduced to a skeleton of dogma, covered with a few rags of casuistry. St. Paul's early mission was to wean the infant Church from this very thing, from a legalistic, moribund Judaism (Gal. 2:16–21). It was the Law of the Spirit, he told the Romans, that ought to free them from the law of sin and death (Rom. 8:10–11). In the mind of St. Paul 'the Spirit gives life' (2 Cor. 3:6), the Spirit Christ left as a divine Person after his Ascension. That is why salvation, brought to us through Christ's Death and Resurrection, is a free gift of new life, made available through all time by the Holy Spirit, freeing the Jew from the bonds of the Law, and the Gentile from corruption, making both children of God (Rom. 8:14–16).

In his vision St. Paul saw that Pentecost had turned the world upside down; for the symbolism of the Spirit had been completely reversed. From the beginning of time it was the Spirit of God who was the irresistible power behind the Word. The Spirit brooded over the dark waters of chaos, when the Word commanded creation (Gen. 1:1–5). It was the Breath of God that stirred 'the wind', that dried up the dark waters of the Flood to free Noah and his family (Gen. 8:1). From the deep mist that separated the Israelites from the Egyptians, 'the wind' of God blew and divided the sea for a safe passage for the people of God (Ex. 14:21–22). The Spirit was 'the dense cloud' that surrounded Sinai, when God proclaimed his Law (Ex. 19:9), his 'strength' that filled all those through whom the divine promises were to be made (Isaiah 40:9). His 'breath' energized the word of God that the prophets proclaimed (Ezekiel 37:5–10). But it was the greatest prophet of all, this 'greater than Solomon' (Matt. 12:42), who received the fulness of the Spirit. No one could say with such truth: 'the Spirit of the Lord is upon me' (Luke 4:18). From his mother's womb, the Spirit had given him the throne of David his ancestor (Luke 1:26–35). He was the one upon whom the Spirit rested, and was proclaimed the Son of God (Luke 3:21–22). And if the disciples in their turn saw him as the Son of God, it was because they saw the fulness of God's Spirit in him (Matt. 16:13–17).

But now the roles and symbols were to be reversed. It was no longer the Spirit who pointed to Christ, but Christ who communicated the Spirit. It was no longer the Spirit who consecrated Christ as Son of God, but the Son of God, at the Father's right hand, who freely bestows the fire of the Spirit (John 20:22). 'I have come to bring fire to the earth' (Luke 12:49), and 'something appeared to them that seemed like tongues of fire... They were all filled with the Holy Spirit' (Acts 2:3–4). It was Christ's mission to enkindle this fire, to warm and evangelize the world with the vitality of his risen life. It was not until then, as St. John tells us, that the Spirit was given: 'Now this he said about the Spirit, which those who believed in him were to receive; for as yet the Spirit had not been given, because Jesus was not yet glorified' (John 7:39).

It may seem strange to us that Our Lord should have used the symbolism of fire to present us with the reality of his Spirit. Yet he was only echoing the voice of Israel of old, and indeed of all humanity, that saw in fire the truth of God's presence. Isaiah foretold: 'The light of Israel will become a fire and its Holy One a flame' (Isaiah 10:17). Fire symbolizes so beautifully the reality of Christ's Spirit dwelling in the Christian soul through Baptism and the sacramental life. But the Spirit can never be born within, as Our Lord reminded Nicodemus, except in the darkness of the night journey, in the darkness of the womb (John 3:3–8). Always the Christian soul comes to new life by way of its own darkness. It is in our own dark journey that we deepen, as best we can, our sense of sin, and come to understand as well a little of humanity's sins and sorrows. St. Paul knew this from experience: 'The fire will test the quality of each man's work' (1 Cor. 3:13).

Fire burns, and the flame of the Holy Spirit is a fire of love, radiating in the within of our being, making us living temples of God. 'Didn't you realise that you were God's temple and that the Spirit of God was living among you?'

(1 Cor. 3:16). The author of the Letter to the Hebrews says: 'Our God is a consuming fire' (Heb. 12:29), and the Christian soul becomes ablaze, enkindling others with the fire of this love. For it is in the fire of our love that we radiate and manifest the Spirit of Christ. St. Paul reminded the Galatians that with the Spirit as their rule of life, they would reap the harvest of the Spirit, and what a harvest: 'a harvest of love, joy, peace, patience, kindness, generosity, forbearance, gentleness, faith, courtesy, temperateness, purity' (Gal. 5:22–23). Above all, it is the Holy Spirit who gives a sense of joy and optimism, that opens the eyes to a vision of all that is revealed in living and loving. St. Luke tells us Our Lord had this: 'It was then that, filled with the joy by the Holy Spirit, he said, "I bless you, Father, Lord of heaven and of earth, for hiding these things from the learned and the clever and revealing them to mere children. Yes, Father, for that is what it pleased you to do" ' (Luke 10:21).

I love that passage, translated by Monsignor Knox, where St. Paul thanks God for the gift of his Priesthood: 'So much I owe to the grace which God has given me, in making me a priest of Jesus Christ for the Gentiles, with God's gospel for my priestly charge, to make the Gentiles an offering worthy of acceptance, consecrated by the Holy Spirit' (Rom. 15:15–16).

11

The next day after this, John was standing there again, with two of his disciples; and, watching Jesus as he walked by, he said, Look, this is the Lamb of God. The two disciples heard him say it, and they followed Jesus   *(John 1:35–37)*

How good God is to give us characters, the Saints, our friends and the people with whom we live, to charm and delight us. Like many another I have always had an attraction for that hero, 'filled with the Holy Spirit' (Luke 1:16), of whom Our Lord spoke so highly: 'I tell you solemnly, of all the children born of women, a greater than John the Baptist has never been seen' (Matt. 11:11). During my twenty eight years in the Monastery, on June 24th the Church bells and the organ music of Pat Collins' Fair could be heard, wafted on the still night's air, as the Parish of Whitwick kept the feast of its Patron Saint, John the Baptist, and I was brought to the reality of the angel's remark to Zachary: 'Joy and gladness shall be thine, and many hearts shall rejoice over his birth, for he is to be high in the Lord's favour' (Luke 1:14–15). Indeed, one cannot herald in the dawn every day of one's priestly life with the words of the Benedictus: 'Such is the merciful kindness of our God, which has bidden him come to us, like a dawning from on high, to give light to those who live in darkness, in the shadow of death, and to guide our feet into the way of peace' (Luke 1:78–79), and not think of John the Baptist, the light preparing the way for one's vision of Christ.

I could see clearly the single, yet twofold movement, immersion and emergence, participation and sublimation, so well outlined in his life. 'As the child grew', St. Luke tells us, 'his spirit achieved strength, and he dwelt in the wilderness' (Luke 1:80). At home in the darkness of the desert, where 'the word of God came upon John, the son of Zachary' (Luke 3: 2), he could appear in the light on the banks of the Jordan, and 'thereupon Jerusalem and all Judea, and all those who dwelt round Jordan went out to see him' (Matt. 3:5). Content to eat 'locusts and wild honey', he could mix with soldiers and tell them not to 'use men roughly' and 'be content with your pay'. Dressed in 'a garment of camel's hair and a leather girdle', he could join company with court circles and rebuke their morals (Matt. 3:1–6 and Luke 3:1–20). The desert indeed was the dust from which 'the new self' was formed.

Today, when reason has subdued nature, St. John cuts a strange figure. Our contact with nature and symbols to a great extent has gone, and with it the profound emotional energy it supplied. But St. John was at home with the wild life of the desert, with the mountains and hills, the windings and rough paths, with the winnowing fan and the threshing-floor, wheat and chaff, with water and fire, trees and their fruit (Luke 3:1–18). It was because of his sense of vision that he saw a dove hovering over the Son of Man and knew he was God's Son. 'Now I have seen him, and have borne my witness that this is the Son of God' (John 1:29–34). Unlike St. John the Baptist we imagine that external reality is presented to us to build up our own integrity. But this is only to scratch at the surface of knowledge. The deeper truth is, that the world draws us into itself to a reality belonging to it, everywhere present to it, but yet more perfect than it. When we are absorbed by the demands of every day life, we seldom catch a glimpse into the deep reality that lies hid there. 'Look, this is the Lamb of God' (John 1:37).

It is the wonderful sense of beauty infused into our hearts by God himself, that makes us see into the reality of things. St. Paul tells us that Christ entered the womb of the world 'to fill creation with his presence' (Eph. 4:10). At every moment he awaits us in his creation. 'Look, this is the Lamb of God'. Christ quickens us with his omnipresence. In the life that springs up within us, in all the material elements that sustain us, in the joy of love and friendship, it is Christ himself we encounter; in our sufferings and failings his hands ever mould us. 'Look, this is the Lamb of God'. St. Mark tells us that when Jesus asked the blind man, Bartimaeus, 'what do you want me to do for you?', he said: 'Master, let me see again' (Mark 10:51). To see Christ in all the ordinary circumstances of life, to see him in a chaste contact with all creation, is the secret of all living and loving. And 'next day, John saw Jesus coming towards him; and he said, Look, this is the Lamb of God; look, this is he who takes away the sin of the world' (John 1:29).

We are told: 'Jesus came from Nazareth, and was baptized by John in the Jordan. And even as he came up out of the water he saw the heavens opened, and the Spirit, like a dove, coming down and resting upon him' (Mark 1:9–10). It is in our own immersion too that we meet Christ and emerge, like him, with the mark of love resting on our shoulders. All living is seeing, and all seeing is loving. Life is creative energy, and in both the Creator and in ourselves love is the one supreme energy. Love is the one link that binds us and all things together, and why we can find it in everything that exists. For 'from him, no creature can be hidden', says the author of the Letter to the Hebrews, 'everything lies bare, everything is brought face to face with him' (Heb. 4:13). Love is suffocated in the impersonal; it is in the Person of Christ that love becomes aflame. 'You are all one person in Jesus Christ' (Gal. 3:28). He is the centre where all things meet. In our embrace with him we hear not only our own cries and prayers, but also the weeping and praying of all our fellow women and men. In Christ we touch their inmost depths.

It is there too we find our differences. John the Baptist's disciples had a dispute with the Jews. Being depressed 'they came to John, and told him, Master, there was one with thee on the other side of Jordan, to whom thou didst then bear testimony. We find that he is baptizing now, and all are flocking to him'. John tried to reassure them: 'A man must be content to receive the gift which is given from heaven, and nothing more. You yourselves are my witnesses that I told you, I am not the Christ; I have been sent to go before him... He must become more and more, I must become less and less' (John 3:26–30). So true is it that Christ consumes. But the paradox is that Christ always builds up again. That Christ may become more part of us, we need alternatively sorrow that brings death, and joy that enlarges the heart. What exhilarates us more than all else is the joy of being possessed by Christ.

Our process of growth and Individuation, as St. John the Baptist knew so well, is a lessening of the old self to 'be clothed in the new self, which is created in God's image, justified and sanctified through the truth' (Eph. 4:24). It is then that Christ is seen and loved, not only as the centre of our being, but also as the fulness that fills the whole sphere of reality. Indeed, the one Christ, who consumes us with his love, is the same Christ, who with the same love, the same presence enters all those around us. Christ binds us and reveals us to one another.

In Christ individuality and personality converge. That is why St. John the Baptist could say to his disciples: 'The bridegroom's friend, who stands by and listens to him, rejoices too, rejoices at hearing the bridegroom's voice; and this joy is mine now in full measure' (John 3:29). It was joy the angel foretold in announcing his birth (Luke 1:13–14), and joy that caused him to leap in his mother's womb (Luke 1:43–44). To grow in joy is to find that joy is a divine gift. Joy uplifts and nourishes, urges us on, and creates undaunted optimism. It was joy that St. John the Baptist proclaimed, joy that comes from vision and loving.

6

I have seen God face to face
(Gen. 32:30)

THE YEARS come and the years go, and the wonderful thing is they leave behind them something of meaning, something eternal. In their restless rise and fall, the waves of time beat relentlessly against the shores of eternity, and leave there what is eternal. Before our deeds fall into nothingness, they give birth to an eternal property.

Pope Paul VI marked the year 1975 as a Holy Year, and dedicated it to renewal and reconciliation. In his Wednesday General Audiences that year he returned time and time again to his theme of 'the importance of personal prayer'. He stressed the need we all have for a spiritual life, and the joy that comes from a personal life of prayer. He deplored the fact that 'today, unfortunately, many people no longer pray, do not pray at all'. The secret of all living and loving lies in the balance of opposites, that brings wholeness to 'the perfect Man, fully mature with the fullness of Christ himself' (Eph. 4:13). God always radiates from himself; with ourselves action blossoms from passion, a fruitful apostolate, a successful life, draws its blessing from a personal interior life.

The year 1975 also saw the centenary of the birth of Dr. Jung. Jung was a remarkable man in so many ways, and a depth of spirituality can be found in his works. After years of contact with patients, he found that few had any interior experience of God. He could also see that the mark of our present age is that of a great expanding, outgoing movement of progress in society. To balance this, he looked to an inward movement and focused his attention on the individual, with a respect and love for the person. St. Paul too was preoccupied with the same thought when St. Timothy was setting out to forward the growth of Christ in the Roman world. He told him: 'Two things claim thy attention, thyself and the teaching of the faith; spend thy care on them; so wilt thou and those who listen to thee, achieve salvation' (1 Tim. 4:16). Jung's psychology led him to an awareness of God's living presence, an awareness that is the true basis for any life of prayer. Like so many of the great spiritual writers of the past he realized that prayer should be much deeper than just saying words. It can be sought in so many ways – in speech, thought and good works, but especially by being still and passive in the presence of God. To remind himself and his visitors of this presence, Jung carved on the lintel of the door of his house at Bollingen the inscription 'To all, the welcome and unwelcome, God is here'.

Time is dynamic and carries us along. There is a rhythm in our lives, and we have to submit to its enthralment. Yet all the time God is at hand, he is present and beckons us on. Our desire to be one with him and possess him finds us at the same time possessed by him. This is expressed so beautifully by St. Catherine of Siena; writing in her 'On Divine Revelation' she says: 'Eternal Trinity, you are like a deep sea, in which the more I seek, the more I find; and the more I find, the more I seek you'. It is an unending process, and the amazing thing is, how in God's providence, we fall upon acquaintances and situations that have just the right influence to help and mould us. It is all God's work in the art of loving and living.